Twayne's United States Authors Series

Sylvia E. Bowman, *Editor*

INDIANA UNIVERSITY

John Crowe Ransom

JOHN CROWE RANSOM

By THORNTON H. PARSONS

Syracuse University

 150

Twayne Publishers, Inc.   ::   New York

To *Doris*

Preface

THIS BOOK is an investigation of one of the five extraordinary vocations that converge in the rich career of John Crowe Ransom. Few American literary men of this century have been as versatile and influential as this poet, critic, teacher, editor, and trainer of young writers. Few have had the force of personality and style to lead movements and institutions as important to American intellectual life as the Fugitives and Agrarians, *The Kenyon Review,* and The Kenyon School of Letters. Only Pound and Williams have had as profound a personal impact upon younger writers; for among Ransom's students are Allen Tate, Andrew Lytle, Robert Penn Warren, Cleanth Brooks, Robert Lowell, Randall Jarrell, Peter Taylor, and Anthony Hecht. Who besides Eliot can match Ransom for prolific output of critical essays consistent with lucidity, point, and rhetorical finish?

In this bustling age of criticism Ransom's prose has been amply examined and assessed, but there have been no book-length studies of his poetry. My exclusive attention to his poetry is designed to compensate for an unjust neglect. Furthermore, I believe that an austere restriction to formal analysis and evaluation of the poems is quite consistent with Ransom's own rigorous esthetic principles, and especially with his critical ideal of the poet's anonymity.

As a poet, Ransom is a virtuoso of covertness. Since his early indulgence in straightforward verse, *Poems About God,* he has been unrelenting in his search for techniques by which to produce poetic effects while securing the author's anonymity. Most of his poems, therefore, invite a critical strictness, an exacting attention to their autotelic design.

To dramatize the persistence and variety of the search, I discuss in Chapter 1 some little-known poems from *Chills and Fever* and *Two Gentlemen in Bonds.* Though a corrective is needed to the undiscriminating praise of those volumes by Cleanth Brooks and F. O. Matthiessen, I emphasize these poems neither as a perverse advertisement of their mediocrity nor as a gratuitous support of Ransom's good judgment in excluding them from his *Selected Poems;* I wish to show how completely Ransom was committed to the doctrine of esthetic distance, and how much fruitless ingenuity he expended upon it.

Furthermore, I reserve the best poems of the early volumes—what will become the *Selected Poems*—for treatment in the next four chapters, which are analyses of the most persistent and durable techniques. My method here is still to accommodate Ransom's apparent poetic purposes, to bring into relationship poems that embody similar themes and techniques, and to discover the kind and degree of success that Ransom achieves. Quotations in these four chapters are from the 1955 paperback, *Poems and Essays.*

The scrupulous standards by which Ransom worked are further manifested in his numerous revisions. Chapter 6 is a canvass of the revisions made for the three versions of *Selected Poems* and an argument for the 1955 edition as the best representative of Ransom's work.

—THORNTON H. PARSONS

Syracuse University

Acknowledgments

By arrangement with Holt, Rinehart and Winston, Inc., I quote from *Poems About God*, and with Alfred A. Knopf, Inc., from *Chills and Fever, Two Gentlemen in Bonds, Selected Poems* (1945 and 1963), and *Poems and Essays*.

The editors of *Perspective, Modern Language Quarterly,* and *Southern Review* have generously permitted me to reprint here articles of mine that they first published.

I thank Syracuse University for a research leave; and I thank James Elson, Sanford Meech, Frank Piskor, and Walter Sutton for their encouragement.

Contents

Chronology

1888   John Crowe Ransom born April 30, in Pulaski, Tennessee.

1909   B.A., Vanderbilt University.

1910–   Rhodes Scholar at Oxford University, England.
1913

1914   Joined the faculty of Vanderbilt University.

1917–   First Lieutenant Field Artillery, U. S. Army.
1919

1919   *Poems About God.*

1920   Married Robb Reavill, December 22.

1922–   Helped to found and edit *The Fugitive.*
1925

1924   *Chills and Fever.*

1924   *Grace After Meat* (London).

1927   *Two Gentlemen in Bonds.*

1927   Professor of English at Vanderbilt University.

1930   *God Without Thunder.*

1931–   Guggenheim Fellow for Creative Writing.
1932

1937–   Carnegie Professor of Poetry at Kenyon College.
1958

1938   *The World's Body.*

1939–   Editor of *Kenyon Review.*
1959

1941   *The New Criticism.*

1945   *Selected Poems.*

1951   Bollingen Award in Poetry (Yale University Library).

1951   Russell Loines Award in Literature (National Academy of Arts and Letters).

1951   Edited *The Kenyon Critics* (with introduction).

1955   *Poems and Essays* (paperback).

1961   Edited *Selected Poems of Thomas Hardy* (with introduction).

1962   Academy of American Poets Fellowship.

1963   *Selected Poems* (a revised and enlarged edition).

1964   Book of the Year in Poetry Award.

CHAPTER 1

The Early Volumes

THE ESTHETIC maturity of Ransom developed rapidly. The good poems in *Chills and Fever* reflect principles that must have been utterly alien to the First Lieutenant Field Artillery, American Expeditionary Force, who published *Poems About God* in 1919. None of the poems of that first publication have survived in any of the three versions of *Selected Poems*. *Chills and Fever* was published in 1924; and, though the poems are uneven in quality, they are not sentimental and moralistic; they are not dull in the way that the *Poems About God* are.

I *The Muse of Directness*

What is most startling about the first volume is that there are not even slight premonitions of the later poetry. Ransom speaks directly and ingenuously, trusting that the reader is as unsophisticated as he and that esthetic pleasure inheres in commonplace events simply and garrulously recited. The work reflects a simple amateurism, a complete freedom from esthetic self-consciousness. It is so guileless and candid that to criticize it seems a harsh breach of faith.

Still, I want to illustrate the completeness of the five-year metamorphosis from a writer of sentimental and banal verse—and even doggerel—to the scrupulous poet operating with rigorous principles, spending energy and ingenuity upon the avoidance of emotional overstatement. In *Poems About God* Ransom works within the convention of sentimentality. He usually speaks personally and directly, and the excuse for a poem is the display of strong feeling. A few lines at the end of "Noonday Grace"— a long, verbose piece of doggerel celebrating the pleasures of food, domestic harmony, and God's providence—illustrate how unguarded the author is:

An extra fork is by my plate,
I nearly noticed it too late!

Mother, you're keeping a secret back!
I see the pie-pan through the crack,
Incrusted thick in gold and black.

There's no telling what that secret pair
Have cooked for me in the kitchen there,

There's no telling what that pie can be,
But tell me that it's blackberry!

As long as I keep topside the sod,
I'll love you always, mother and God.

The iambic meter is either too rigid or too loose; some lines reflect an unabashed sacrifice of the meter to a dubious rhyme.

"Sunset" is a long, unrhymed poem with no discernible metrical pattern. It is bad prose arranged in lines to give the appearance of verse. The perilous objective of this work is to depict a girl who is preoccupied with her closeness to God, her attraction to infinity. A straight presentation, it is an earnest and direct poem. Even the animals are treated with sober piety. Cows are given an imagined speech:

Cropping the clover are several spotted cows.
They too are kind and gentle,
And they stop and look round at me now and then
As if they would say:
"How good of you to come to see us!
Please pardon us if we seem indifferent,
But we have not much time to talk with you now,
And really nothing to say."
Then they make their bow,
Still kind and calm,
And go their way again
Towards the sunset.
I suppose they are going to God.

Fanciful invention goes unchecked. Next, the dog is credited with a civilized restraint:

Rover!
O here he is, waiting.
He has chased the rabbits and run after the birds
A thousand miles or so,
And now he is hungry and tired.
But he is a southern gentleman
And will not whimper once
Though you kept him waiting forever.

In many of the *Poems About God* fancy is at work in the
service of the sentimental convention. Devotion to fancy is the
one trait that Ransom will carry over to his new practice of a
detached and disinterested poetry. *Chills and Fever* and *Two
Gentlemen in Bonds* abound with whimsical conceptions, innocuous little poems that seem crudely 'made up' and not developed
in the heat of passionate discovery and insight.

Even the irony found in *Poems About God* is so obvious that
it supports Ransom's sentimental purposes. It is not used as a
way of securing detachment but rather as a way of increasing
shrill outrage. A very discursive poem, "Grace," is a denunciation
of the undignified way in which a humble and pious hired man
succumbs to death. The narration is primitively direct: "I'm
thinking now how he was saved/One day while plowing in the
corn." The heavy irony of "saved" is made apparent later with
these lines, designed to show how simple piety may be rewarded:

> Sundays, the hired man would pray
> To live in the sunshine of his face;
> Now here was answer come complete,
> Rather an overdose of grace!
>
> He fell in the furrow, an honest place
> And an easy place for a man to fall.
> His horse went marching blindly on
> In a beautiful dream of a great fat stall.
> And God shone on in merry mood,
> For it was a foolish kind of sprawl,
> And I found a hulk of heaving meat
> That wouldn't answer me at all,
> And a fresh breeze made the young corn dance
> To a bright green, glorious carnival.
> And really, is it not a gift

To smile and be divinely gay,
And rise above a circumstance
And smile distressing scenes away?

God is derelict for permitting the disparity between the bright weather and the agonizing death. Very realistic descriptions follow: both the hired man and the narrator vomit, and the hired man dies in this sordid and repugnant state.

Irony is used in "A Christmas Colloquy" to illustrate the cruelty of a country minister who seeks to displace his daughter's interest in Santa Claus with the story of Christ's birth. To provide a quaint narrative plausibility, Ransom has the conversation between father and daughter overheard by a dog. A bolder ironic idea is developed in "Worship," only to be repudiated by a trite moral at the end:

I know a quite religious man
Who utters praises when he can.

Now I find God in bard and book,
In school and temple, bird and brook.

But he says God is sweetest of all
Discovered in a drinking-hall.

For God requires no costly wine
But comes on the foam of a crockery stein.

And when that foam is on the lips,
Begin then God's good fellowships.

Cathedrals, synagogues, and kirks
May go to the devil, and all their works.

And as for Christian charity,
It's made out of hilarity.

He gives the beggar all his dimes,
Forgives his brother seven times.

"I love the rain," says thirsty clod;
So this religious man of God.

For God has come, and is it odd
He praises all the works of God?

"For God has come, and there's no sorrow,"
He sings all night—will he sing to-morrow?

This concluding line ruins the fresh unconventionality of treatment and suggests that the young Ransom was a timid ironist. Ill at ease with the unorthodox character he had created and reluctant to give the appearance that he endorsed so racy a celebration of God, he betrayed his characterization with a pious didacticism.

II   A Sophisticated Poetics

The first poem in *Chills and Fever* dramatically announces the change in principles. *"Agitato ma non troppo"* is an explicit rejection of emotional overstatement, and the poem's execution is quite different from anything in *Poems About God*. It is a highly appropriate introduction to *Chills and Fever,* for all of these poems reflect Ransom's effort to avoid the gross heresies of sentimentality, overstatement, and naïveté. In the poems of 1924 are signs of an intense self-consciousness about poetry, and I am afraid that many of them are interesting mainly for this reason. The ostensible purpose seems to be to make them as remote from the poet's feeling as possible. Often trivial and whimsical subjects are presented with an elaborate attention to tone, and only rarely can Ransom generate even an intellectual excitement from them. Ingenuity of sophisticated detachment can become a paltry substitute for intense feeling. So, great as the differences are between *Poems About God* and *Chills and Fever,* the two volumes are related in their lack of important personal discoveries as the basis of poetry.

Few critics have been as bold as Robert Lowell in proclaiming that Ransom is not a minor poet. This condescending designation is adopted by F. O. Matthiessen and is implied by several other critics as they set about defending Ransom on the grounds of "elegance," "traditional sensibility," or "classical decorum"—attributes that are praiseworthy only when they are found in company with a powerful intensity, when they work unobtrusively to heighten that intensity. Edmund Wilson calls Ransom "A Water-Colorist."

Many critics have noticed the persistent theme of the divided sensibility in Ransom's poetry, but few have made much of the precedence which Ransom himself gives to the intellect in his implicit preference for tone over emotion. Sentimentality has been as much a tyrant for Ransom as for Hemingway; fear of it and ingenious effort to avoid it have produced many sterile and innocuous poems.

One sure way of avoiding sentimentality is to write about a weatherbeaten legendary character far removed from the interest of author or reader and, though her plight calls for pathos, to treat it with a mocking tone. In the title, "Rapunzel Has Submitted Herself to Fashion," Ransom hints at a farfetched treatment. Then from a great emotional distance he chides the victim:

> Rapunzel, and Rapunzel,
> All this day will I cry upon you,
> Accusing, Was it well
> How the old witch has enviously undone you?
>
> Undone of your tangled snare
> By which the midnight moon was sifted and stranded;
> Forlorn of the rippling stair
> Whereon the secret lover had ascended.
>
> For when it came to night,
> And the breath-shortening of the most shut hour,
> Should he have mounted light
> And delivered you with a kiss, and possessed the tower.
>
> But the beldame spat between
> The crooked blade of shears,
> And put her warty hands to the sheen
> Of your hair, and hacked it off, and maybe hacked your ears.
>
> Do you sit at the casement still,
> Braving the ruins of your smile but wanly?
> Prince there shall come not till
> He may climb to his kiss on a rippling ladder, only.

It is very hard to see that any plausible esthetic intention has been fulfilled here. The details of the legend are rehearsed but not given a fresh turn or a modern relevance. Novelty consists entirely in the detached attitude and in the rather perverse and self-conscious will to be fanciful about Rapunzel's destitution and frustration.

In *Chills and Fever* Ransom turns again and again to this strange practice of the pointless fanciful elaboration. "On the Road to Wockensutter" tells the story of Brady, whose philosophical eccentricity is to reduce the variety of existence to the single "Principle of Venus." On a march through a desert he sees a pewit and, sure that the bird is another embodiment of Venus, declares his wish to shoot it, though he doubts that he could kill a supernatural creature. Eight stanzas of this nonsense are the incredible preparation for the ending:

> "And though I had a miracle of salt
> To sprinkle on your saucy tilt of tail,
> I think I'd rather loose you in default
> Than catch another mere obscene female."

In "Boris of Britain," a protracted narrative, an alchemist effects a miraculous transformation in a patient who complains of an ailing head, and invests him with a rare legal talent—the ability to detect false witness. Boris is supernaturally carried to court where he argues a case and becomes so angry at a lying defendant that he assaults him and some of the officials, causes a riot in the court, and is disbarred. Inevitably, the ending is anticlimactic:

> Boris, a single-minded man,
> Has turned an honest publican,
> With a preference for quiet
> But an aptitude for riot;
> Serves the trade without deceit
> And shows the merry ones the street;
> And as for the lass named Nellie—no man
> Has a helpfuller woman.

It is a perplexing elaboration of a lame drollery.

Unrewarding as the innocuous design may be, it is a persistent interest in the practice of the reformed Ransom. "Grandgousier," "Youngest Daughter," "Winter's Tale," and "The Vagrant" belong with this group. In "Grandgousier," the farcical account of a dying man who wants to enjoy drinking to the end, the conflict is created by Bishop Bamboozle who sanctimoniously forbids the maids to serve anything except ice water and thus keeps the old sinner from a last glimpse of the illusory Paradise he has known:

Will you give him to guzzle,
Bishop Bamboozle,
A sponge from a jar
Of the rank vinegar?

For to sip where he lies
Till he ups and dies—
And this is his day—
Till the pink puffed eyes
See the old Paradise
Of the Grandgousier.

The obvious difference between this poem and "Worship" is that Ransom dares to preserve here a sophisticated ironical perspective; but that alone does not lift this dubious conception into poetry.

"The Vagrant" depicts the town idiot, who is considered harmless because his imagination is filled not with lustful desire for the local girls but with visions of the beautiful women of romantic literature. I suppose this portrait may be taken as an ironical one of the poet whose motives are so different from those of practical men. Whatever promise the idea might have, though, is overwhelmed by the crude versification, obvious rhyme, and flat language. Ransom likes so well the folksy description, "a bee in his brains," that he uses it twice.

"Winter's Tale" presents the story of Drury, a man who lives in passive isolation with his cats until "Tom the Tawny" leaps out of the window and leads Drury to Jenny, his mistress. Thus is Drury "corrected/Of being long a ninny."

"Youngest Daughter" tells of three suitors of a girl named Heart's Desire. The first is a sailor who is "seduced by her ill-bred lady-in-waiting." The second is a burgher who is distracted by "her tidy scullery maid." The third is the scholar who is found "compromised with a musty tome" in the library. For revenge on the three, the mother swears that her daughter will never wed.

A slight variation of the fanciful narrative is the undeveloped conflict. The implausible effect is to leave the reader without inclination either to like or dislike, to sympathize with or scorn, the character presented. "Number Five" is the mysterious designation for our narrator, one of five "hang-dog men" or "thirsty pirates." He is with his desperate companions in a tavern, but

"I couldn't drink to my mates, lest I might speak." As the proprietor and a girl fix their attention upon him, he fears that he will tell what dreadful act he has committed. So he goes out in an open field and howls in the storm.

The undeveloped and unresolved conflict can be a dialogue between two pompous speakers. In "Night Voices" Christ and Nicodemus debate whether human beings should be given the hope of immortality. Each is dogmatic and immovable; so there is really no drama. Nine stanzas prepare for this anticlimactic and equivocal modulation to atmosphere:

> And further on they walked,
> Out of old passion in the heart they talked,
> And when the grey morn glimmered overhead,
> They found they trod the gardens of the dead,
> And spectre-white they stalked.

An impoverished ambiguity is worse than none at all.

"Fall of Leaf" is a longer, more turgid dialogue, between Dick and Dorothy, "Summer foresters." That the reader may easily recognize who is speaking, each artificial speech begins with direct address: "Dorothy, the year's played out"; "Dick, the play is done for them." As they speculate about aging ("Dorothy, we grow no younger"), courses of action are proposed. Dick suggests that Dorothy can go to an eastward gate; then she identifies the place as a nunnery and says that she would not be accepted there. Dick suggests that they both can go to a westward gate; again Dorothy identifies the place—a monastery—and says that a mere woodman (Dick) would not be acceptable to the monks.

> "Dorothy, then will you tell
> The way that goes from Lovers' Hell?
> All the potent charms are said,
> We that clasp are cold and wearied;
> Heartless lovers are as dead
> That walk the earth unburied."
>
> "Dick, they found the ending good,
> The Babes that ventured in the Wood.
> So tell the leaves that die and fall,
> As we lie a-shiver,
> Stop and stitch us one close pall
> To hide us deep for ever."

The implication is clear: Dick and Dorothy will suffer death because they are creatures of time. Ransom follows a wordy and pretentious route to so banal an idea. It is a skeletal version of the theme of "The Equilibrists"; it is an allegory of the choices available in an existence of changefulness—asceticism or "Lovers' Hell."

These are the least engaging of Ransom's strategies for achieving impersonality, and nothing redeems them. Not only do they lack the impact that might come through witty and ironic extension or through metaphorical and rhetorical embellishment, but they lack even the minimal charm of stories told for sheer narrative interest. Emotionless poetry that excludes a rudimentary play of mind is hopeless.

The subtle method of "Winter Remembered" is clumsily used in "Spring Posy," an effort to praise a woman by the sheerest indirection, by the slightest allusion to her:

> Running to meet us came neighbours' daughters nigh,
> Fluting like birds, and calicoed bright and clean;
> And beautiful else had been their bosoms poutering by!
> "But ye are a cloud," I said, "too much between."
>
> I was waylaid in a depth of woody grot:
> Was it a fox in his fern, was it a wing's blue sheen?
> In her widow's weed the balsam? But how ye prospered not,
> When full of her images I saw not your scene!
>
> Up once I rose in a fury of heard-of things
> To travel the splendid sphere that twirleth in its fame;
> But the wars and ships and towns, and pestilent roaring kings,
> These angered me, and why? They fought unknowing her name!

The speaker wants to suggest that his consciousness is so exclusively filled by devotion to the woman that he cannot attend to other lovely and momentous sights, and he is even resentful of possible distractions. The success of this design—praise rendered indirectly—depends upon pleasurable effects along the circuitous way. But, where the reader should find deftness of execution, he finds Ransom's poetic machinery: the absurd diction—"nigh," "beautiful else," "ye"; the attitudinizing—"Up once I rose in a fury of heard-of things"; the extravagant phrasing—"waylaid in a depth of woody grot," "how ye prospered not," "the splendid sphere that twirleth in its fame," "pestilent roaring kings." With the extension of the image of birds, "bosoms poutering by," an alien note of comedy enters. Ransom's pompous mannerisms give the poem a 'manufactured' quality and undermine the emotion that is claimed in it.

When Cleanth Brooks encounters fustian in "Vaunting Oak," he attributes it to Ransom's desire to ridicule grandiloquence; and thus a formidable clog is swiftly transformed into a sophisticated virtue. My theory is less charitable; I too believe that Ransom was struggling for a subtle effect from language, but one of magniloquence. He sought a very suave and elusive control. Heightened language would absorb the attention of the reader, distract him from the author's private personality. That Ransom could achieve the desired effect only infrequently produces one of the persistent ironies of *Chills and Fever*: the zealous efforts to cultivate an anonymity often have no more striking result than to make the reader aware of the poet desperately trying to conceal himself behind eccentric language.

A more pleasurable kind of 'manufactured' poem is the conceitist "Triumph." There is some suspense at least about whether the elaborate analogy will succeed, whether the parallel between the Roman army and the suitor can be made good:

> Athens, a fragile kingdom by the foam,
> Assumed the stranger's yoke; but then behold how meek
> Those unbred Caesars grew, who spent their fruits of Rome
> For ever after, trying to be Greek.
>
> I too shook out my locks like one born royal;
> For she dissolved in tears, and said my barbarous name,
> And took my oath, she was so piteous and loyal:
> Vote the young Caesar triumph, spread his fame!
>
> But oh, I find my captive was not caught.
> It was her empty house that fell before my legions;
> Of where her soul inhabits I have conquered naught;
> It is so far from these my Roman regions!

This design has some promise for a virtuoso of indirection. A frustration can be objectified. Ransom begins by suggesting the ironic plight of the military conqueror who discovers that he does not have an intrinsic superiority but must subordinate him-

self to the finer culture and humanity of the conquered. If the
entire poem were of the quality of the third and fourth lines of
the opening stanza, it would be an admirable work. But Ransom
could not suppress his pedantic and stilted language: "by the
foam," "Assumed the stranger's yoke," "behold." The artificiality
gets heavier just where a graceful pivot should be made: "I too
shook out my locks like one born royal." We see how aggres-
sively the conceit is being urged when the marriage ceremony
receives military overtones. "Barbarous name" is too patently an
echo of "unbred Caesars," but "young Caesar" is unforgivably
overt. In the final stanza an excellent line—"It was her empty
house that fell before my legions"—gently sustains the analogy
and implies a husband's desolate knowledge that there has been
no marriage of true minds. Then the belaboring resumes with
"conquered" and "Roman regions."

"Triumph" is a cold-blooded experiment in the conceitist convention. Nobody can believe for a moment that the poem orig-
inated in emotion, but the ingenuity does afford an intellectual
pleasure, if a pleasure seriously mitigated by persistent obviousness and by not very disarming language.

The first of "Two Sonnets" has a clever idea but a laborious
presentation. So the feeling is academicized. The climax of the
poem is the unexpected turn given to a man's vanity. As a man
and his wife are embracing before a fire on a rainy day, he
thinks he detects a coldness, a detachment, in her. However,
when she chides *him* for his coldness, he is suddenly elated and
assumes the demeanor of a haughty lover who is willing to relent
for the woman's sake and abate his splendid egoistic isolation;
he magnanimously sympathizes with a deprived person and
gives her his rare emotional attention.

Probably the worst lapses are the trite hyperbole to describe
the man's original melancholy sense of disharmony and aliena-
tion, "thus we might have sat/Till angry Gabriel trumpeted for
change," and the woman's incredible speech: "'Heart of stone,
look not like that!/O unconcessive husband, you are strange.'"
Another line overdoes the man's newly discovered sense of superiority: "The chidden wonder of women, the huge I!"

"April Treason" is based upon an ironical idea. Its conclusion
is designed as a revelation of the diverse emotional quality
which an erotic experience may have for the two people sharing

it. A standard conflict is presented: a painter would like to be true to his art but is overcome by his passion for the girl who models for him. The poem does not unfold suspensefully. There are hints that Ransom worked again from a preconceived idea and went about doggedly and rigidly executing it. The third stanza overtly forecasts the approaching temptation:

> He had nearly done his portrait,
> But there came a day in April;
> There was treachery come winging
> On the dust of flowers springing;
> It was not a day for artist to play host
> Lest the man come uppermost.

This poem is a curious mixture of floridity and flatness. Every stanza has some extravagant phrasing like that of the third and fourth lines here, and the very turgidity ought to have some justification. But it does not. The aim was rhetorical heightening. If Ransom were after a playful effect with his rhetoric, the poem should not have the sober, even grim, progression to the thematic irony. If we take the excesses of language as Ransom's implicit ridicule, then we must know what the target is. Is it the theme? Is it poems on this theme by other writers? A deliberate grandiloquence can serve no function in this poem. The emotional disparity emphasized at the end is a serious matter, and it would not be a sensible strategy to develop it through flippancy.

After the artist has succumbed and "kissed her lips," he disgustedly destroys the picture, his art which he has betrayed. Here is the melodramatic description of this act:

> Then for all his giddy pulses
> He laid grim hands on the picture,
> And he trampled it with loathing,
> Flung it many miles to nothing,
> Till it screamed to wake the devils as it fell
> Till it thundered into hell.

The bombast is unintentional; it results from a too-explicit design to make the reader feel the man's powerful self-disgust, and to prepare for the irony of the ending, when the vapid girl reduces

the artist's mighty sense of self-betrayal by saying, "It was nice!"
She is far from intuiting his response to their adventure:

> Then a silence straightway took them
> And they paced the woodland homeward.
> What a bitter noon in April
> (It was April, it was April)
> As she touched his fleeting fingers cold as ice
> And recited, "It was nice!"

"What a bitter noon in April" is itself superfluous, and we see
how relaxed the esthetic standards are when Ransom adds the
bland embellishment of the next line.

Even when Ransom is clearly fashioning a satirical portrait,
as in "Nocturne," he begins with a rhetorical prodigality:

> Where now is the young Adam, sultry in his Aiden?
> And where is the goat-footed, pursuing his naked maiden?
> Our man shall cut few capers in his dark seersucker coat,
> His grave eye subduing the outrageous red tie at his throat,
> Considering if he should carry his dutiful flesh to the ball,
> Rather than open his book, which is flat, and metaphysical.

Inflated, bookish epithets for spontaneous, primitive man tele-
graph the motif of contrast, make it too stark. They do not evoke
a feeling for the innocent sexual freedom enjoyed by the early
ancestors of our man in the seersucker coat. The language reflects a contrivance so blatant that I do not know how a reader
can consider it and still cooperate sympathetically with the
poem. The tax upon the reader's magnanimity is similar to that
often imposed by the expression of Swinburne and Poe.

Ransom's 'intellectual' poems are more substantial than his
droll narratives. Their genesis may be attributed to an imaginative engagement of central human existence rather than to a
blithe indulgence of whimsy; thus they have a more permanent
interest for us. Their predominant flaws do, however, remind us
of the author's unflagging loyalty to a program of antisentimen-
tality; for, while Ransom seeks to avoid the obviousness of shrill
emotion, he succumbs to a counterdistortion—obviousness of
rhetoric. The poems have a fabricated quality because the language is not felicitously suited to the subject, does not work in
quiet and gentle subordination to theme; instead, it makes an

autonomous claim upon the reader's attention, a claim quite independent of the meaning.

Tireless experiment with detachment leads Ransom to a more astonishing disparity than that between subject and rhetoric. In "Miss Euphemia" not grandiloquence but terseness predominates. The apparent movement is toward an impact of tonal novelty; Ransom tries to produce a surprising and telling effect from his sheer severity of detachment upon a pathetic subject. "Miss Euphemia" resembles "Conrad Sits in Twilight" in purpose and tone, if not exactly in method.

Although the plight of a frail and deprived old spinster seems to call for pathos, Ransom keeps undermining it. She "crept" from her house—"her winter's gaol"—expecting to be revivified by the newly arriving spring. She is a prisoner hopefully "Out of the frore escaping/To the blue upper arch." The use of color helps to establish the incongruity: the earth was green "But white upon her stick went/Miss Euphemia...." Then with a brusque and too-efficient narration Ransom has her fleeing from the spring, returning to her house and her chair. In the final stanza, a counterpart to her physical weakness is described: she has no capacity for imaginative hopefulness.

> Nor scarcely can she, dwindling,
> Throw down a bridge of dream
> For a broken lady's traverse,
> Neat-footing on the beam;
> She had too much of winter,
> And all her ways were lost,
> And she sits with us only
> Till next Pentecost.

Ransom stays safely away from this lady's sensibility. She is described from the outside. "Dwindling" and "broken"—cold adjectives to apply to a human being—are the austere preparation for the serenely objective figure, "She had too much of winter," and for the callous conclusion. As the last two lines cannot be read as a thematic consummation of the poem, their great effect is to remind us of a poet stolidly practicing his detachment. Any ingenuity that requires so willful a denial of *appropriate* sympathy is too expensive. The poem offers no justification for reducing Miss Euphemia to an object that is merely reported on.

Ransom is able to generate a greater suspense about his tonal control when he implies a personal relationship, when the fiction of the poem forbids a cold detachment like that in "Miss Euphemia." Because "To a Lady Celebrating Her Birthday" calls for a personal effect, the reader can feel a dramatic interplay between subject and tone. Ransom must ask a greater versatility of himself, for subtlety demands that he somehow obscure his predicament, his dilemma of motives in trying to wrest a personal tribute from a detached presentation. But the versatility is a thin one. This poem has an unusual development: two abrupt turns suggest that Ransom either grew impatient and despaired of a uniform tone or trusted that the modulations could convey a restless refinement of feeling.

A Donnean image in the opening lines is used to compliment the woman: the sun looks in at her; he shows signs of having aged during the past year, but she does not:

> Too quick the annual sun returns,
> Mounts to the ledge and scans the pillowed face
> Whereon four seasons hardly have writ the trace,
> Though even he on his timeless circuit mourns
> That faintlier his fire burns.

This conventionalized hyperbole is followed by a conventionalized list of durable materials that are appropriate gifts to celebrate beauty: "topaz, emeralds, gold, and minerals rare"; "Musk"; and "Bright stiff brocades." Spiritual qualities that can be constant—"kind affections"—are also appropriate gifts, but "trembling flowers" are not, because they are emblems of mutability, a point given wordy emphasis in this stanza:

> But bring no gift of trembling flowers:
> Dear comrade, never on pain of pain suppose
> From the blowing of any little wasted rose,
> Up clomb the enemy in the airy towers
> To number beauty's hours.

There is some hope at this point that Ransom will suddenly elevate his poem and transcend the mediocrity of the first two stanzas. He could use as a dramatic pivot this bold denial that the lady's beauty is subject to the enemy (time) in the way that flowers are. We might expect a brilliant Neo-Platonic casuistry now.

Instead of a bewildering display of verbal power, Ransom gives us a flat reversal, a colorless truism:

> Ah, but I think you clearly know:
> Sure eyes, you have observed on what hard terms
> Beauty has respite from voracious worms;
> Her moment comes; thereafter fast or slow
> Her daily funerals go.

The obvious distinction is that a woman's beauty is not afflicted as suddenly as a flower's is. "Daily funerals" suggest a slow attrition. So we are not to have the pleasure of a subtly extended sophistry.

Next, unpredictably, the woman is urged to "rise up and proudly sing," to ignore the danger from the enemy as soldiers do the night before a battle, and to revel as the Babylonians did even when they saw their imminent destruction. These exaggerated imperatives are very misleading, for the next stanza affirms a disinclination to overstate:

> Small, small, my heart inclines to boast:
> What can a virtuous poor pale lover do
> Who's prey to dissolution quick as you?
> This day smells mortuary more than most
> To me upon my post.

This shift is as capricious as the preceding one. The reckless exuberance of "rise up and proudly sing" is harshly negated by "This day smells mortuary...." And in the last stanza all lyric hyperbole is abandoned for grim, stark realism:

> Know this, though desperate our cases:
> Thus will I hold you out of other harms
> Till these be palsied paralytic arms;
> Then be we grizzled polls and yellow faces
> In these respective places.

We have been led a strange and crooked journey to this direct pledge of constancy. If surprise is one of the effects of this poem, it is not the admirable kind—wonder at the wit and verbal agility of the poet—but dismay at the capricious and dissolute shifts of tone.

III *Whimsy, Irony, and Metamorphosis*

Circumvention of personal emotion continues to engage Ransom in his third volume, *Two Gentlemen in Bonds,* published in 1927. Again the cost of the circumvention is usually too high; detachment is won as a proper end in itself, not as an impressive control of strong feeling or startling insight. The work that supplies the title to this volume is an arduous story of two brothers —one ascetic, one worldly—presented in twenty sonnets, which must be Ransom's most complete indulgence of his love of the cool, fanciful narrative.

This sonnet sequence is a bizarre combination of whimsy and irony. The serious theme—that temperamental one-sidedness dooms each brother to restless unfulfillment and to utter failure of sympathy for his kinsman—is presented ludicrously to prevent the reader from identifying with the characters. The brothers are really caricatures: one committed wholly to the bodily pleasures of eating, drinking, riding, love-making; the other to the intellectual pursuits of reading, writing, introspecting, dwelling constantly upon death and human vanity. While one brother is exerting himself to entertain the king, the other absents himself and broods in the tower. Licentious shallowness and sterile gloom are the respective fates. The irony of the beginning is the irony of the ending: in the final sonnet the deceased father of the brothers speaks and laments the splitting of his whole sensibility into the two disjunct offspring; but, as nothing can be done about it, he concludes that he might as well return to sleep.

After we have made our way through these sonnets, we find no illumination, no dramatic point to justify our cooperation. Too much weight falls on the story itself, a very obvious and dull story, with little touches of whimsy along the way (one digression, for example, "Epithalamion of a Peach"—meant to be extravagantly amusing—describes the eating of a peach in the language of sexual ravishment). There is no charm of incident, no acute revelation of personality, no startling verbal or metaphoric ingenuity, no movement into satisfying philosophic point.

The volume *Two Gentlemen in Bonds* has one kind of bold experimentation not to be found in *Chills and Fever.* Ransom tries to produce metamorphoses, poems that could conceivably accommodate his strange addiction to whimsy and yet have a zestful impact. The esthetic effect aimed at is surprise.

"Jack's Letter" carries symptoms of a willful effort to write a 'metaphysical' poem. It is based upon an absurd conceit, the sort that might be inspired by a reading of "The Flea" by Donne. A man who is intent upon writing a love letter and who despairs of conveying his emotion by words *plants* "Himself in bulbs of cunning charactry" on the paper and counts on the woman's tears falling on the sheet to make the bulbs grow. A sophistical salvation might be won by a gracefully ingenious attenuation here, but the ending has a resolute obviousness:

> Here then lies Jack beneath a penny seal.
> The dainty lady of the superscription
> If she have very delicate perception
> With eyes may see and with sharp fingers feel.
>
> The post is gone, and the event will tell.
> If only she should lay it to her bosom,
> Her parcel might soon thicken to a blossom
> Which would be soft to hold and sweet to smell.

When ingenuity runs so wild, the best that the reader may hope for is not a transcending of the absurdity with a semblance of emotion for the man's plight, but a cool pleasure in some deft and startling extension; and, when even that is lacking, the poem is appalling.

"Husband Betrayed" has a less outrageous fiction. A man who playfully gives his wife the nickname "Pigeon" discovers that it has a horrifying relevance, for she turns out to be lazy and incapable of properly returning his love. Something could have been made of this idea, but Ransom sabotages it with pompous language and a ludicrous tone. Most of the unfortunate commitments are made in the first stanza:

> And so he called her Pigeon,
> Saying to himself, "She flutters walking
> And in sweet monotone she twitters talking."
> Nothing was said of her religion.

The feminine rhyme, the implausible diction, and the trivial tone are persisted in to the end. Shaky control is foreshadowed in the hopelessly farfetched line, "Nothing was said of her religion."

The metamorphosis, which should be revealed suddenly at the end, is thumpingly insisted upon:

> At all events she had a snowy bosom
> And trod so mincingly that you would say
> She only wanted wings to fly away,
> Easy and light and lissome.
>
> She pecked her food with ravished cries,
> She sunned her bosom by the wall in the morning,
> Preening prettily in the sun and turning
> In her birdwise.

After such heavy foreshadowing, there can be no deft, sudden revelation of the metamorphosis; so the ending is anticlimactic, a ponderous effort to complete the obdurate design:

> But there was heavy dudgeon
> When he that should have married him a woman
> To sit and drudge and serve him as was common
> Discovered he had wived a pigeon.

An even more amorphous version of this motif is "Amphibious Crocodile." What surprise there is in it is exhausted in the first two stanzas:

> In due season the amphibious crocodile
> Rose from the waves and clambered on the bank
> And clothed himself, having cleansed his toes which stank
> Of bayous of Florida and estuaries of Nile.
>
> And if he had had not water on his brain,
> Remember what joys were his. The complete landlubber
> In a green mackintosh and overshoes of rubber—
> Putting his umbrella up against the rain. . . .

With this explicit account of Robert Crocodile's origins Ransom can too easily allude to them when he wants to suggest that the persistent reptilian instincts frustrate all the man's efforts to do anything properly human. The American dilettante clumsily samples dissipations, then travels to Europe. Paris suggests sensual indulgences to him, but he can be distracted even from them by his brutal interest in the scene of World War I. When he arrives at a trench, the "green slime and water" make him nostalgic for his previous state, and he longs to shed his clothes. In England, he ineptly tries the pleasures of riding a horse in the country and lecturing at Oxford; then he dabbles in religion, psychoanalysis, and philosophy. But the pull of the prehistoric instincts is too strong; and he returns to America, takes off his clothes (shunning the disciplines of humanity), and lets himself go:

> Full length he lies and goes as water goes,
> He weeps for joy and welters in the flood,
> Floating he lies extended many a rood,
> And quite invisible but for the end of his nose.

The work has too cumbrous a machinery for satire; it is a piece of doggerel.

The only poem of this group that Ransom has salvaged for his *Selected Poems* is "Lady Lost." It alone has the gentle, charming, unobtrusive movement toward surprise. The motif is not given away at the beginning, for the reader can take the first stanza as precise and meticulous description:

> This morning, flew up the lane
> A timid lady bird to our birdbath
> And eyed her image dolefully as death;
> This afternoon, knocked on our windowpane
> To be let in from the rain.

This projection of a human mood upon a bird poised over its reflection in the water does not seem contrived or farfetched; nor does the assumption that the bird might be distressed by the rain. The precision and projection are continued in the second stanza:

> And when I caught her eye
> She looked aside, but at the clapping thunder
> And sight of the whole earth blazing up like tinder
> Looked in on us again most miserably,
> Indeed as if she would cry.

Now Ransom is ready to make the sudden leap that the reader is almost ready to believe in because he has been gently induced to cooperate with an analogy, or, more precisely, with what he could innocently assume to be an analogy:

> So I will go out into the park and say,
> "Who has lost a delicate brown-eyed lady
> In the West End section? Or has anybody
> Injured some fine woman in some dark way
> Last night, or yesterday?"

The dainty movements and the sad-eyed timorousness of the bird can be swiftly associated with a gentle, vulnerable woman; and the modest metaphysic of surprise has been realized. But, in the stanza that Ransom adds to attenuate the effect, he manages only to belabor the metamorphosis. Overtness produces not a finer delicacy for the reader to savor but an anticlimax: "'Let the owner come and claim possession....'"

We have three versions of *Selected Poems* for evidence that Ransom's experiments with an austere poetics were not always so slender in achievement. From *Chills and Fever* and *Two Gentlemen in Bonds* were mined most of the formidable poems that have secured his reputation and that we have yet to examine.

CHAPTER 2

Civilization and Sympathy:
The Poems about Death

THIS CENTURY has produced uncompromising enemies against the provincialism of America. John Crowe Ransom is a worthy parallel to T. S. Eliot. They are to American poetry what Henry James was to American prose. They are advocates and practitioners of a civilized poetry; in them culminate the esthetic subtlety and scrupulosity that the obdurate American character resisted for so long.

Civilization is primarily a matter of emotion and what to do with it, how to have it: spontaneously and powerfully, say some, fearing the possible tepidness of decorum; ritualistically and controlledly, say others, fearing anarchy and enthusiasm. The two cardinal traits of a thoroughly civilized person are the positive desire for emotional poise and the negative dread of naïveté. When the civilized person functions as a conscientious writer, he is likely to cultivate the literary traits of urbanity, wit, irony, tact, tone—to be, in short, highly self-conscious about emotion and, at the same time, intensely alert to conceal this self-consciousness. Irony and wit save a good deal of the predominantly romantic American literature from naïveté; they pervade the writings of Melville, Emerson, Hawthorne, Thoreau, and Frost.

Eliot's differentiation between vague and precise emotions is an important one for the poems of John Crowe Ransom. His poems are most successful when the emotion is clear and definite, when a certain shade or nuance is captured, when the right pitch is achieved. While vigilantly seeking to avoid too much emotion for the circumstances, Ransom sometimes evokes too little. A great part of the pleasure in reading a poem by Ransom issues from the suspense in waiting to see whether, as the poem unfolds, he will be able to manage the fiction so that a precise emotion will emerge and converge with theme and characterization, and whether the perspective is right to justify the tone, the inevitably appropriate attitude. This is the subtle pleasure of an intense and patient leisure.

Ransom's is a poetry of poise. It demands a language formal enough to avoid rawness, coarseness, obviousness; yet not so formal that the emotion is frozen out. It demands a perspective that will permit the emotion to emerge impersonally, but will not provide an excessive detachment that seems nonhuman. It demands wit and irony that will control the tone, but not degenerate into flippancy and pale neutrality. A highly civilized poetry draws its strengths from the virtues of civilization and runs the risk of achieving only the parodies of these virtues.

Ransom has eight poems about death that reflect the subtle powers and the subtle flaws of his esthetic conscience. The subject of death attracts poets for different reasons. The sentimental and the disillusioned can extract an easy self-pity from it; the tough and the sophisticated can practice their detachment upon it. Changes of taste in poetry dramatize the perils of extremes. As an aversion to formalism can increase the danger of emotional overstatement, so an aversion to sentimentality can increase the danger of a tame and passionless detachment. A poet's troubles are perennial. When the techniques for avoiding raw pathos become obtrusive, the poem may develop a chilly aloofness toward legitimate human feelings. Though the emotion in reading is esthetic, power comes from the reader's sense of a possible relationship between the fictional emotion induced by the work and the real emotion that individuals feel in their private lives. The ability to be affected by illusory emotion originates in the susceptibility to an analogous emotion that might be experienced in the flesh.

In the Classical revival that Hulme prophesied and that we have had in this century, nobody—not even Eliot—has been more consistently wary of direct personal emotion in poetry than Ransom has since his first book. The success of his kind of poetry must depend largely upon the invention of fictions that will accommodate his values, that will permit the convergence of plausible emotion and theme with mode of presentation. His poems never fail because of overstatement and naïveté; the perils he

approaches are tameness and contrivance. The virtuosi of directness usually have emotion—sometimes too abundantly and sometimes too rawly. Ransom's urbanity and decorum impel him to
place tone and perspective very high in the hierarchy of esthetic
values, and occasionally his checks against effusiveness and sentimentality diminish the emotional impact of his poems. In other
words, his poise fails. Sometimes, in refining out the impurities,
he sacrifices some of the power. In each of his most successful
'death' poems he has discovered a fiction that elicits a precise
emotion in a dramatic way: in one, a proper mode of psycho-
logic control and behavior is played off against its contrary; in
another, the funeral ceremony of a woman becomes an ironic
substitute for the marriage ceremony; in the other two, the
deaths of a boy and a girl are treated from fresh perspectives.

I   *Only Atmosphere*

Two unsuccessful poems about death illustrate Ransom's willingness to pay exorbitantly for esthetic distance. "Piazza Piece"
and "Necrological" have static characterizations; the characters
are presented so thinly and with such neutrality that the prob-
lem of sentimentality is frozen out from the start, is not even
relevant to the poems. In "Piazza Piece," a very slight poem,
death is implicitly treated through the convention of courtship,
but without richness, without data to arouse any sympathy for
the young lady. She is as conventionalized and static as the
elderly suitor, the allegorized Death. Probably the best stroke
is the witty phrase, "gentleman in a dustcoat": Death protecting
himself against dust. There is a good movement from the delicate
ears of the young lady to the roses on the trellis. Parallel mutability is gently suggested. There is some complex synaesthesia
in "the spectral singing of the moon"; the pallor associated with
death is converted to an audible reminder of the destruction that
awaits beauty and youth. The speech of the young lady—with the
exception of one phrase, "grey man"—is flat. This phrase echoes
the color symbolism of Death in a dustcoat and of a deathly
singing through the pallor of the moon. "Truelove" is an obtrusive addition to the conventionality of the poem, the conventionalized emotion.

Because the young lady has no particularity, no individuality,
we cannot empathize her plight with any sharpness. If any emo-

tion is generated in the reader when an allegorized Death reminds a generalized woman of the perishability of her youth, it must be a stock response, an excessive willingness to cooperate with the inadequate data of the poem. So the poem exists mainly for its atmosphere; it is an exercise in esthetic virtuosity. We may admire its language, but its impoverished fiction does not invite an intense participation by the reader.

"Necrological" is somewhat richer, but the deliberate guards against emotion make it solely an 'atmosphere' poem, too. Ransom has an elaborate apparatus for maintaining esthetic distance upon the subject of death: a safely medieval narrative, archaisms, a matter-of-fact tone for describing grim and horrible sights, a neutral character limited to a passive registering of the macabre scene.

This poem is suffused with the feeling of death, conveyed by sharp, precise, visualizable details. A somber mood is quickly established with the friar's ascetic ritual; he said his paternosters and scourged himself, then meditated—but not calmly: "with much riddling his head became unruly." As he left the monastery and made his way to the nearby battlefield, he saw the dead men by the light of dawn. Here Ransom uses the imagistic technique of associating color with deathliness. Dead men had been stripped of their clothing by their slayers, and the stark dawn light showed their bodies "whitely bare." The great number of dead men is suggested by the white cast which the bodies impart to the whole field, "white like meads of asphodel"—a fine Miltonic hyperbole. Then by a precise distinction another color also associated with death is used to refine upon the chilling whiteness. The corpses were not entirely white, for they had been bloodily despoiled by "the grey wolf." By this simple contrasting of red and grey Ransom controls the tone of this stanza, and enhances the horror while keeping it indirect. An unreal, eerie quality is further sustained by the word "fabulous."

Bartholomew, who led the victorious soldiers and wrought all this death, is not himself free of death. As a soldier, he is inextricably connected with it and is always in danger of being killed. Thus the mood of death is extended even to the victor, preventing any cross-current from arising to check the poem's movement toward a wider and stronger sense of deathliness.

The grim panorama is completed by two sharply drawn pictures contrasting the warmth and passion of recent life with the irremediable chill of present death. The dawn's blue sky frames a couple in an ironic posture, a grief-stricken leman clutching the knees of her dead warrior. It is like sculpture. An attitude of love in life is now an attitude of grief in death. Their lost vigor as a couple is suggested by his "mighty" knees, and her "flame" that had "warmed his tent." To complement this motif of contrast is the picture by the sable stream of the white horse and its rider. The word "spilled" is excellent for conveying the precariousness of the life substances that support man and beast. "The great beast had spilled there his little brain,/And the little groin of the knight was spilled by a stone." Brain and groin, the seats of life, are shown in all their fragility.

The poem ends with a quiet climax, a delicate extension of the deathliness, as the friar identifies himself with the corpse-heavy landscape and, in imagination, blends into it. His consciousness is absorbed by the sights of death, and he becomes thoroughly at one with deathliness.

Ransom was not satisfied, apparently, with the indirectness that he could achieve through the use of characterization. He enhances the indirectness by investing the friar with a neutrality, a pale anonymity, that limits the intensity of anything he feels. In this poem Ransom seems to be refining upon detachedness as much as he can, for even the data registered by a neutral character are presented in a formal language that dulls their impact: "Flesh fails, and the postured bones lie weather-beaten"; "The lords of chivalry lay prone and shattered." This language *sounds* very good, very dignified, very elevated; but it is spoken from such a great emotional distance that we do not credit the friar's discomfiture, we do not feel the emotion of a particularized character. Ransom's mournful rhetoric has "sublimed away" the personal anguish.

Ransom's technique in these minor poems is to subordinate characterization to atmosphere. The young lady and the friar are props for an esthetic exercise, and the emotion of the poems is restricted to esthetic pleasure in a neutral effect, similar to the pleasure derived from Imagist poems. It is inaccurate to say that Ransom avoids sentimentality in these poems, for he shunts the reader away from any exciting interest in the personalities of the characters; they are generalized, diffuse, remote.

II *Incompatible Perspectives*

He takes greater risks with emotion in "Janet Waking" and "Here Lies a Lady." Attention is focused on somebody who is learning about death in one, and on a dying person in the other. Because these poems induce a sympathetic feeling for the characters involved, Ransom must exert a more ingenious tonal control. He is resourceful in his effort to avoid an excessive and obvious emotional reaction to death; but the ingenuity in both poems is obtrusive. It breaks the illusion. This is the paradoxical trap of the self-conscious Classicist: he may assert his private personality (or at least make us aware of it) by an overscrupulous effort to achieve esthetic distance.

"Janet Waking," a poem about a child's difficult and painful awakening to the reality of death, is preserved from obvious pathos by an alternation of perspectives, a little girl's and an adult's. The opening is effective not only because of the different meanings of "Beautifully" but because of the unusual syntax. "Beautifully Janet slept" is fresh for the same reason that Frost's line is: "Something there is that doesn't love a wall." Put both clauses in normal word order and they are flat. "Dainty-feathered hen" gives us the child's delicate appreciation of her pet. But the adult perspective comes in with "To see how it had kept." "Kept," with its implication of mutability, has a touch of humor that would be foreign to Janet's single-minded interest in the hen, the exclusive interest implied in the adult's description of Janet's perfunctory attention to members of her family. The third stanza's dazzling metaphysical image, "Running across the world upon the grass,/To Chucky's house," returns us to Janet's perspective. Then in the next two stanzas the adult (probably Janet's father) presents a cool and ludicrous account of the way Chucky died. Janet's emotion must be held in abeyance as we respond to the comic diction: "transmogrifying," "droning down," "old bald head," "sat and put the poison." After this strong draught of grotesqueness, we resume Janet's simple point of view: "And weeping fast as she had breath/Janet implored us, 'Wake her from her sleep!'" The poem's last two lines combine both perspectives: "And would not be instructed in how deep/Was the forgetful kingdom of death." Now the tone is quite serious, as the pathetic plight of the child is described; but the adult is there to keep us from a simple identification with her.

This combination of pathos and comedy is perhaps Ransom's least subtle and least effective way of controlling the emotional response of the reader. The comic perspective of the adult interferes with the appropriate pathos which we know the child feels at discovering the permanence of death. When two perspectives simply appear side by side in the poem, the effect is to blur the emotion, to annihilate the integrity of the poem. Emily Dickinson ends a poem with these grimly comic lines: "You will know I'm trying/With my granite lip." But this is comedy that subserves the emphasis of the poem: the enormous difference between life and death, between a lip that once was mobile and capable of utterance and a lip that has assumed a dreadful immobility like that of the monument a few inches above it.

In the weakest lines of "Janet Waking" the comic view is carried so far into absurdity that the reader completely loses touch with Janet's traumatic sadness:

> It scarcely bled,
> But how exceedingly
>
> And purply did the knot
> Swell with the venom and communicate
> Its rigor! Now the poor comb stood up straight
> But Chucky did not.

The parallelism of "purply" with "exceedingly" is amusing, and so is the bloated rhetoric to describe the swelling and poisoning; but, combined with the bad joke about the erectile comb, these touches are too lighthearted. The poem fails because of its implausible fiction. If the narrator is the father of a girl receiving her first awareness of death, he should not be capable of so much flippancy. For the complexity and sophistication of this poem Ransom has paid with a disunity, with a diminution of the central emotion—a Pyrrhic victory at best.

Ransom's technique for tonal control in "Here Lies a Lady" parallels that of "Janet Waking," except that there is no identifiable narrator and the pathos is alternated not with comic absurdity but with cool detachment, distanced reporting. Suspense issues from the first line: the reader wonders what Ransom is up to in his combination of the conventional elegiac phrase,

"Here lies a lady," with the somewhat stilted "of beauty and high degree." Will he combat the standard sentimental response with a formal tone? The next line suggests that his strategy will be more complex than this. At first, we take the "high degree" as a reference to social status; but the second line makes us see it retroactively as a pun, referring also to temperature: "Of chills and fever she died, of fever and chills. . . ."

The chiasmus is a versatile device here. It supports the pun in creating detachment from the lady, but it paradoxically works against the pun to keep the tone from becoming flippant. This technique of retroactive coloring appears again: "The delight of her husband, her aunt, an infant of three,/And of medicos marveling sweetly on her ills." "Delight" is a peculiar word here, but it has warmth when it is ascribed solely to the husband or the infant, possibly even the aunt; but, when it carries over to the impersonal "medicos," it is diminished in all its applications. So, after reading only the first stanza, we are puzzled to know how to feel about this woman. Is the subject of death not to be taken seriously? A great apparatus for esthetic distance has been created before any pathos has entered the poem.

Pathos enters, however, in the second stanza; rather, it is induced very deftly by Ransom. Meticulous description of the feverish woman's pointless activity, of her furious but futile busyness, makes her plight very moving. In this highly successful stanza, a strong pathos is generated without overstatement, without any obviousness.

> For either she burned, and her confident eyes would blaze,
> And her fingers fly in a manner to puzzle their heads—
> What was she making? Why, nothing; she sat in a maze
> Of old scraps of laces, snipped into curious shreds. . . .

This is our greatest emotional proximity to the woman. The movement from this point in the poem is toward detachment.

In the description of the chill, our feelings toward the victim are controlled by the objective reporting and by the choice of an analogy that emphasizes inertness. The pathetic furious victim of fever abruptly is reduced to a lifeless object "like a thin stalk":

Or this would pass, and the light of her fire decline
Till she lay discouraged and cold, like a thin stalk white
    and blown,
And would not open her eyes, to kisses, to wine;
The sixth of these states was her last; the cold settled
    down.

After the emotionality of the preceding stanza, "the light of her fire decline" comes with a jarring, obtrusive formality. The third line only underscores the incapacity to respond as a human being; and "the cold settled down," while a more successful modern idiom and metaphor for death than "a gentleman in a dustcoat," is an astonishingly cool report of a death, as impersonal as a scientist's report of a stage in an experiment.

"Here Lies a Lady" ends with an attitude so devoid of emotion that it is disconcerting. First, the address to the "Sweet ladies" is so impersonal that we utterly lose touch with a specific personality who has suffered an illness leading to death. Archaic language and self-conscious rhetoric increase the already excessive aloofness. Then comes the bizarre question, "But was she not lucky?" And I am puzzled to know the identity of the questioner. This vagueness about the narrator is the poem's central flaw. There is no consistent perspective that the reader may evaluate. The perspective that would yield the most intense emotion would be that of the woman losing her life, that of the husband, or that of the child. But Ransom chooses to end the poem with a tone so cold that it seems nonhuman. This austerity may be consistent with the poem's many detached and objective effects, but it seems like a contrived flight from the legitimate human emotion that we are invited to share in the second stanza. In combating the sentimental elegy, Ransom has been caught in the countertrap of callousness and nonhuman detachment.

Is the lady lucky to be relieved of the oscillations between pointless fury and cold inertness? Is she lucky to die with people around to mourn? Is she lucky to have so symmetrical a death? *She* did not bloom long; *she* did not thole toughly. The poem has a remarkable inconsistency of feeling; the shifts in tone are too contrived.

III   *The Narrative Reflectors*

In "Emily Hardcastle, Spinster" Ransom is able to effect a

much more satisfying compatibility between emotion and esthetic decorum. He does so by a brilliant use of euphemism as a structural device. The poem is entirely built on a dignified and elaborate euphemism: the ceremony of death is presented metaphorically as the ceremony of marriage, not with strain and far-fetched ingenuity, but with economy and compressed relevance.

Perspective is consistent and plausible, and admits of a legitimate emotion; for the narrator is one of the men in this town who had hoped to woo and marry Emily Hardcastle. His regret and grief are sedately conveyed with a rhetorical formality and a palpable rhythm:

> We shall come tomorrow morning, who were not to have her love,
> We shall bring no face of envy but a gift of praise and lilies
> To the stately ceremonial we are not the heroes of.

Rhetorical formality is buttressed by a ritual formality: "the stately ceremonial." This phrase suggests the marriage ceremony that some of the men would like to have been "the heroes of." "Heroes" is an excellent indirect way of pointing up forcefully the regret of the narrator and other would-be suitors of Emily, and it hints at her superhuman standards. The marriage ritual is exploited throughout the rest of the poem. This emphasis is appropriate because the interest in marriage defines the narrator and provides the plausible excuse for his response to the death; and the interest in marriage defines Emily Hardcastle, the protagonist. Her sisters can *now* attend her as they would have if she had married, but the emotion—not of joy in marriage, but of grief in death—is implied in the description of them as "red-eyed" and "wroth." Marriage is used to contrast Emily with her sisters. Though she was the oldest daughter, she refused to compromise her standards in order to marry. Her two sisters did; they cynically or shallowly married "merchants."

The motif of marriage is continued in the third stanza. A high-spirited youthfulness is conveyed by the narrator's description of himself: "I was dapper when I dangled in my pepper-and-salt." This is a subtle nostalgia. The amusing jauntiness of "dapper" and "dangled" and "pepper-and-salt" is tonal preparation for the facetious wistfulness of "local beauties," the description of the young men who "beautifully trusted" that Emily would have to relent, to abate her scrupulous standards and accept one of them. Ransom's language in this stanza carries some very elusive feelings. The young men were a little cynical: they doubted their own worthiness; they doubted that Emily could ever find them exemplary of her ideal; and they doubted that Emily could persevere in her idealism if it meant spinsterhood. Their casual cynicism is nicely summed up in the line: "If the proud one had to tarry we would have her by default." It is a rich stanza, defining the young men and differentiating the "finer" Emily from her sisters and from the casually complacent suitors.

The ending registers the ironical value of a woman's high standards for love and for marriage. Someone from 'away' comes to claim her, someone of rank—not a local beauty; but he has not the courtliness of the gentleman who took another Emily for a carriage ride. This Emily has not been rewarded with the gentle suitor her idealism deserved; her caller is a "Grizzled Baron." The poem ends with a precariously balanced attitude: Emily has been true to her idealistic standards, but she has husbanded this excellence only for Death, who doesn't know how to value it. The euphemism is preserved in the casting of Emily as a gentle princess. "Wrap" and "seal" are subtle and efficient words that support the metaphor of the match between the rough baron and the gentle princess (*wrap*: dress well for a cold journey; *seal*: give over or assign permanently), but they also suggest burial.

This poem has an admirable unity. Irony is inherent in the predicament of Emily Hardcastle; it is not brought in for the sake of toughness; it is built into the poem's structural metaphor. Marriage is not an extraneous subject brought in for esthetic expediency or mere cleverness; it is the most effective way of revealing the plight of a particularized woman, her suspension between two alternatives, neither one entirely satisfactory: spinsterhood with standards, or marriage with compromise.

Though the poem generates pathos for the lost warmth and fulfillment of the woman and for the failure of human life to accommodate an ambitious idealism, the pathos has rich insulation in the persistent detraction from the funeral service by the appropriate talk about marriage. Furthermore, death is not so terrible when it comes to put an end to the frustration attending dreams of excellence that cannot be fulfilled. This poem achieves a delicate poise between what people want and need and what they can have. It is like Emily Dickinson's "It might be lonelier without the loneliness." Theme, emotion, and perspective converge brilliantly. The technique is sure: Ransom revitalizes the treacherous rhetorical device of euphemism and makes it evoke a sense of sadness and waste; the device softens, that is, it permits Ransom to take a step back from the starkness of death; it permits indirection yet creates an intensity of feeling.

'Barbarous' Dylan Thomas says, "Rage, rage against the dying of the light." His poem invites a blurring of actual experience and fiction, and has a very crude perspective designed to elicit strong emotion immediately: a son (indistinct from Dylan Thomas) feels the monstrous injustice of his father's dying and expresses the raw human wish that death could be transcended or effectively fought against or renounced. The mature Ransom would never succumb to this blatancy. When he writes about death, he wants above all to avoid wonder at anything so pervasive and so inevitable. His method for controlling the emotion in "Dead Boy" is to give the multiple responses to a particular death, to show it in a configuration, to depict the different degrees of grief and the different motives that elicit grief and sorrow in the survivors. His method of preserving freshness and originality is to concentrate upon a subdued, elusive grief that is not often dealt with in poetry.

As the narrator of "Dead Boy" is apparently a distant relative who has come to the funeral, he is plausibly free to register and report the different intensities of grief and the various reasons for it. The opening is remarkable for its quiet announcement of the poem's motifs, for the extraordinary amount of information deftly packed into it, and for the scrupulous attitude which it sets for the whole poem. "Foul subtraction" is a good example of Ransom's successful 'metaphysical' language. The outrage implied in "foul" is swiftly tempered by "subtraction," implying an emotionless, impersonal force that cuts down human life. This tonal complexity is much more satisfying than the straight indignation of Thomas' poem. Paradox is appropriate to capture the balanced feelings of the narrator, who resents the fact of death but who will not give up complexity and immerse wholly in indignation.

"Transaction" provides an intensification of the horror of

death, a quietly understated chill. "A green bough from Virginia's aged tree" introduces an esthetic suspense as we wonder how Ransom can save this figure from its tired associations. The rest of the stanza makes the distinction between the members of the family who live in that county and those from farther counties or other states. "Outer dark" carries the attitude of the local people, a sense of the vague and mysterious geography of provincial people. This precise distinction is sustained by the words "none" and "some," and its importance is clear by the end of the poem. It is an admirable stanza.

Now follows some effective rhetorical parallelism:

> A boy not beautiful, nor good, nor clever,
> A black cloud full of storms too hot for keeping,
> A sword beneath his mother's heart—yet never
> Woman bewept her babe as this is weeping.

There is a low-keyed directness in the quick glance at the boy's appearance, behavior, and talent. This line is followed by two striking metaphors that establish his lamentable temperament—his tantrums, the power to torment. Then comes the paradox of the mother's extraordinary grief, which isn't so paradoxical when we remember that even a negatively active child registers himself in the consciousness of adults more strongly than a mild one does. The boy had no attributes that would mitigate the ugly temperament.

Factual reporting of the mother's grief in the setting of paradox allows the reader to feel the powerful emotion without being coerced by it. Then the narrator delivers his shocking metaphor for the boy alive, a description that diminishes his significance even more than "black cloud" and "sword" had done:

> A pig with a pasty face, so I had said,
> Squealing for cookies, kinned by poor pretense
> With a noble house. But the little man quite dead,
> I see the forbears' antique lineaments.

He was so disreputable to an objective observer that it seemed he could not have belonged to this admirable family. But, lying immobile in the casket, he does resemble his ancestors. The language here is subtly toned. "Little man" is complex: it has the usual aura of mawkishness and adult condescension, but it reflects too the narrator's polite deference for the mother's grief, his willingness to soften his judgment under the circumstances; and it gently pivots the poem into the dynastic theme of the last two stanzas, from the narrator's perspective a more important reason for lessening his old disapprobation. This "little man" does belong to them, for he has in the immobility of death "the forbears' antique lineaments." Now the precise emotion of the poem is established: the emphasis is upon the grief of the sterile old men of the family, a grief they do not reveal as outwardly as the mother reveals hers.

"Box of death" is like "foul subtraction" in its restraint that releases a powerful sense of horror. "O friendly waste of breath!" is the perfectly concise line for funereal small talk. These men are restrained, ritualistically discussing the local news and gossip in order to avoid a direct and indecorous confrontation of raw grief in one another. "Deep dynastic wound" is probably the best phrase in the poem. The elder men wanted the ancestral line to continue, and this boy was their only hope.

In the conclusion are other local responses to the boy's death:

> He was pale and little, the foolish neighbors say;
> The first-fruits, saith the Preacher, the Lord hath taken;
> But this was the old tree's late branch wrenched away,
> Grieving the sapless limbs, the shorn and shaken.

Neighbors, who have no emotional investment in the boy, and who do not have the imaginative sympathy of the narrator, can dismiss this death easily. The Preacher has a standard metaphor designed to comfort, and he delivers it in scriptural language. Here, though, is the poem's most ingenious stroke: the narrator now has a good excuse to modify the Preacher's tired metaphor and thus return to the figure of the family tree and its young branch, and end the poem by gathering in the implication of "antique" in the third stanza. The elder men of the family are sapless and palsied, unable to beget more heirs; and the line will die out. In this redemption of the family-tree cliché Ransom has achieved an inspired combination of strong pathos and decorous expression.

Ransom keeps "Dead Boy" free from sentimentality by sustaining a fiction that allows for a consistent undermining of the boy's character or intrinsic importance. The use of the narrator from "outer dark" is a meticulous justification for this severe objectivity at a time when standards usually melt into the general sadness. (In "The Death of the Hired Man" Frost manages this effect by slyly keeping Warren from seeing Silas before some of his negative traits have been lodged with the reader.) Ransom steers the emphasis away from the most immediate and obvious kind of grief, the most unqualified kind. When he has the narrator speak of the mother he uses formalized, archaic diction: "bewept her babe." This is a way of diverting the reader's sympathy from the mother. Her grief is merely one datum in the whole configuration; her attitude is presented with no more emphasis than is the narrator's, the neighbors', or the Preacher's.

The narrator is precisely right for this poem. He is Ransom's fictional device not only for avoiding raw and excessive emotion but for registering a certain kind of grief. He is imaginative enough to understand a motive that is not his own, a legitimate human motive for a powerful grief that is not dependent upon the boy's intrinsic worth. The interest of the old men in the disreputable dead boy transcends his temperament, character, and appearance. So the emotion of the poem feels authentic. It is won not by exploiting the obvious regret over the sheer fact of death, but by giving the sense of a particular boy in a particular context, and by intensifying the highly selective grief of the old men: their regret that transcends mere personal loss, their heightened sense of mortality dramatized by the cessation of an ancestral line. Their quiet, deeply aching regret is very elusive; and Ransom has conveyed it admirably. Emotion is enhanced, and not overwhelmed or diminished, by technique. Fiction and perspective are consistent; the narrator is free to tell the truth about the boy and yet to feel what his death means to others.

A plausible fiction sustained by an exactly appropriate narrator accounts for the parallel success of "Bells for John Whiteside's Daughter." "Little body" in the first line is perilously close to obvious pathos, but this effect is counteracted by the word "speed," which begins an important motif. The reader's accruing sense of loss in "Dead Boy" is gleaned through the negative impression of the narrator, and a similar technique is used in this poem. The narrator, again, is capable of a considerable emotional distance from the death. He is astonished at the *quietness* that can come over, has come over, the little girl whose energetic noisiness had disturbed him so much.

"Lightness in her footfall" is a delicate suggestion of gracefulness—a quiet way to make the girl attractive before the parallels to "speed" are brought in. She was graceful, but she was vigorous and clamorous even when playing by herself. The conceit of warfare conveys this emphasis: "Her wars were bruited"; "she took arms against her shadow"; she "harried" the geese. The narrator's annoyance by the rude disturbance of placidity is projected upon the geese, "Who cried in goose, Alas." The lovely, gently surrealistic image of serenity—geese presented as a diaphanous snow-cloud passively dripping whiteness on the grass, geese that have "noon apple-dreams"—is abruptly dispersed by the indefatigable girl who converts them into scuttling, goose-stepping soldiers.

Here is a rich and complex controlling of the tone. The finely attenuated feeling of harassment in the narrator is achieved by hyperbole—an extravagant figure for peacefulness followed by an extravagant contrasting figure for clamor. This is the narrator's central memory of the dead girl: her enormous ability to shatter placidity. It justifies the use of the word "Astonishes." It is hard to credit the stillness of the little girl now in the coffin.

Precisely chosen language is the elusive strength of the concluding stanza. Direct statements about the dead girl are terse and restrained, and the horror of death is implicit. "Brown study" is an effective euphemism for death because it has an ironic relevance to the personality of the girl alive; during her energetic life, the quiet, pensive mood seemed as unnatural for her as now seems the reality that so much clamorous liveliness could be permanently stilled. "Vexed" is exquisitely attuned to the narrator's emotional perspective. He is not outraged, not overwhelmed. He was resignedly distressed by her noisiness when alive, and he is resignedly distressed by her temperamentally unnatural repose in death. The implication is that death itself is *vexatious* to human beings. This is close to our usual attitude toward it, our recurring sense of uneasiness that our lives logically imply deaths some time in the future; and, though we grow accustomed to the inevitability, it is vaguely annoying.

The motionlessness of the violently active girl has made her survivors motionless, has "sternly stopped" them, has made them confront death directly and definitely. "Primly propped" ends the poem with the emphasis upon the unnaturalness, the excessive formality, of the girl's appearance. This phrase conveys quietly and implicitly more horror than an indignant outburst would. It is the culmination of a strong and clear pathos that has been won by deft indirection; it is pathos under control, arrived at by dramatically working through the data of speed, energy, noise—and the awful vacuum left by death.

A little girl's death could readily entail a crude and trite pathos, but Ransom skillfully avoids it by limiting the reader's view of the girl to the narrator's version of her. A vivid picture of her in a characteristic moment of her life is presented in language formalized enough to keep us detached, to keep us from empathizing her persona purely: "the tireless heart within the little/Lady with rod." The adult's perspective upon her is consistent to the end. There are no technical 'tricks,' as in "Janet Waking" and "Here Lies a Lady," to damage the fiction and to remind us of Ransom's decorous vigilance or vigilant decorum. The fiction is superbly integrated with a consistent perspective. The technique subserves the evocation of an appropriate pathos.

In Ransom's best poems about death the technique of screening the data through a narrator is very important. These last three have narrators that we are expected to trust. Their perceptions are sure; their emotions are scrupulously appropriate. Ransom's extraordinary versatility is reflected in a delicate attenuation of this technique in the poem, "Puncture." Here the narrator has the right emotions but not in an acceptable way; we have to take him somewhat ironically. This is an inspired internal complexity to give the poem. The narrator is himself a dramatic character whose very effusiveness of speech and behavior contributes to the theme and emotion of the poem, and to the reader's awareness of the civilized Ransomian values implied.

Both atmosphere and character are revealed suspensefully: "Darkness was bad as weariness, till Grimes said,/'We've got to have a fire.'" This statement might suggest a possible relief from the oppressive but as yet undefined circumstances until we read the rest of the stanza and discern the reason for the narrator's reluctance to have a fire: dead men are hereabouts, and the fire would make their forms visible. The terse statement of Grimes is a good introduction to him, and the narrator's stilted phrasing provides a sharp contrast:

> But in that case
> The match must sputter and the flame glare red
> On nothing beautiful, and set no seal of grace
> On any dead man's face.

"Set no seal of grace/On any dead man's face" is an excessively formal and circumlocutory way of saying that corpses are not attractive. It is preparation for the narrator's rhetorical speeches to Grimes.

The firelight leads to the discovery of Grimes's secret by his companion: "I looked at Grimes my dear comrade and startled/ His look, blue-bright—and under it a wound/Which bled upon the ground." A little later in the poem we realize that Grimes is startled because he has hoped not to reveal that he has been wounded. These men are soldiers, and the cause of their weariness is implicit: they have just survived a battle.

The dying man's short sentence, "No, it's an old puncture.../ Which takes to bleeding sometimes," contrasts with the narrator's nervous wordiness:

> "Why, Grimes, I never knew your mortal blood
> Had wasted for my sake in scarlet streams,
> And no word said. A curse on my manhood
> If I knew anything! This is my luck which seems
> Worse than my evillest dreams."

Because Grimes knows that he is dying and because he will not deceive himself, he resists the offer to bandage him, and *indirectly* emphasizes the futility of it by his attempt to distract the other with the grim suggestion that the dead men be ministered to instead. When we read the longest speech of Grimes, we are ready to appreciate his extraordinary courage, calmness, and poise—his use of irony even while dying:

> "Get away. Go work on the corpses, if you wish,
> Prop their heads up again, wrap their bones in,
> They were good pious men.
>
> "But as for me I have the devil's desire
> For delicate tobacco in my pipe, and leisure
> To stretch my toes in comfort by this fire.
> Amuse yourself then some way, find some pleasure
> Sleeping, or digging a treasure."

These are the last clearly audible words that Grimes speaks before he dies; and they reflect his serene ability to detract from his own plight, his ultimate civilized consideration for another person in shifting the subject to tobacco and leisurely comfort by the fire. In the greatest crisis of his life Grimes is not at the mercy of regret, frustration, and bitterness. His psychology is not sweetly benign, though, but toughly ironic.

In the narrator's response to the tough prescription for amusement we see what a versatile perspective Ransom is working with, what complexity and tonal control he manages through a pompous man capable of the right feelings:

> I could not find it. It was too melancholy
> Sitting by Grimes my fortress who reared his head
> Breached in the left wall, and subsiding slowly
> To the defunctive posture of the stained dead
> That now not even bled.

"I could not find it" is an excellent ambiguity. It suggests a too-literal response by the narrator, but it is a nice understatement of the impotence and frustration of anybody who doesn't know what to do while a person he loves and reveres is dying. Because the narrator is given to formal rhetorical expression, Ransom can justifiably get the effect of distance while expressing something that is deeply moving. The strong, courageous, and restrained Grimes—the rare civilized man—is about to blend with the corpses. From the perspective of the adulatory comrade, Grimes's courage and strength are suggested by the conceit of the fortress. And the elevated language (that seems too detached in "Necrological") is dramatically effective here: "and subsiding slowly/To the defunctive posture of the stained dead/That now not even bled."

Ransom has achieved what the civilized poet values: the expression of intense emotion in a pattern of restrained language. When we can bring the personality of Grimes into relationship with "the defunctive posture of the stained dead," the effect is immensely chilling. This is as powerful a sense of deathliness as Ransom creates in "Necrological," but here he has a fictional plausibility for his delicate effects. Two characterizations are unfolding. Something important is going on to justify the attention to setting: Grimes's values are being defined by his behavior while dying, and those values are being authenticated in the way they stand by him during this emotional crisis.

One of the surprising turns of the poem is the pathos we feel for the narrator in his need to do something when no action is appropriate:

> I, not to weep then, like a desperado
> Kicked on the carcasses of our enemies
> To heave them into the darkness; but my bravado
> Quailed in the scorn of Grimes; for even these
> Were fit for better courtesies.

We understand his enormous admiration for Grimes and his overwhelming sense of an imminent great loss. We know why he behaves so barbarously. Nevertheless, he cannot be excused for his outrageous violation of the "courtesies." The delicate climax of the poem is prepared for:

> Blue blazed the eyes of Grimes in the old manner—
> The flames of eyes which jewel the head of youth
> Were strange in the leathery phiz of the old campaigner—
> Smoke and a dry word crackled from his mouth
> Which a cold wind ferried south.

Though Grimes is very near death, he responds to an enormity; he rebukes his companion for desecrating the corpses. Grimes's last word is uttered in the service of emotional poise, in a dramatic defense of appropriate emotion and behavior.

This poem is a superb objectification of Ransom's values rendered with power. Emotion is generated by the subject of emotional control, and the subject is embedded in a rich and complex fiction, in a dazzling convergence of characterization, atmosphere, values, and technical virtuosity.

These eight poems about death reveal the central struggle in Ransom: proper gentility and chivalric politeness are at war with his desire to be cruelly witty on subjects that have been treated too reverently or too sentimentally, subjects that have been off-bounds for lightness and humor. The poems were written over forty years ago, when self-conscious modernism demanded a strong anti-Victorian stance. Four of them are dated because in the divergence between technique and emotion they protest too much; they succumb to archness. "Piazza Piece" is stillborn because no empathy can be generated for the stagy allegorical personae. The fiction collapses. "Necrological" is confined to an Imagist effect because individualized characterization is curbed. The toughness of "Here Lies a Lady" and "Janet Waking" was a novelty forty years ago; in these poems John Ransom is combating excesses too self-consciously, making points against trite and sentimental poetry. But the other four death poems have a permanence, and in their admirable convergence of emotion and artfulness they deserve rank with the best of civilized poetry. In these the modernist technique is used to subserve legitimate human emotion and not to subvert it.

CHAPTER 3

Meagerness and Metaphor:
The Poems about Love

IT SEEMS inappropriate and misleading to speak of Ransom's love poems. They are poems about love that have modernist technical guards against obviousness, naïveté, and sentimentality. None of them has the passionate, reckless immediacy that we expect of love poems; only two of them have an unqualified commitment to the one emotion that precludes forethought and deliberation. All of them reflect Ransom's conscientious aversion to directness and to revelation of the author's private personality and his faith in distance-creating techniques, his determination to hold the reader at a psychological remove from the emotion and from the imaginary people involved. Some of them are cool —almost philosophical—studies of the opposed human inclinations toward passion and toward restraint in the name of some idealism; some of them reflect a queasiness toward love, a reluctance like Prufrock's; some of them trade on a rather thin irony; some of them have local excellences but no culminating realization of the whole; a few of them succeed.

Love is a subject that a self-consciously 'modern' poet would have to try. So many excesses have been committed in its name that he would like to demonstrate that it can be treated without effusiveness, without a slovenly tenderheartedness. But it is never enough merely to avoid the gross poetic heresies of overstatement and sentimentality. The law of compensation operates in esthetics. A poet may win his subtlety and toughness of sensibility only with an implicit emotional coldness or timidity, or with an obtrusiveness of method. The civilized artist must resist his own peculiar susceptibility to the counterheresies of callousness, smugness, and poetry-by-formula. He can get involved in a very delicate economy of thematic and tonal balances, of emotional commitment and artistic scruple.

Ransom's experimental boldness takes an unusual form: the aim is to work with emotional meagerness and transform it. Ransom tries for a startling freshness in wresting a victory from sparsity, in subduing intractable materials and making them serve implausible ends. His is a poetics of voluntarily incurred disadvantages.

There is a ready-made distance available to a poet who decides simply to withhold his commitment to the emotion and emphasize an irony. Cutting across the emotion with irony entails a handicap, though: the poet must work the more ingeniously to create an excited response in his reader. Ransom likes to assume sometimes that love and honor are irreconcilable. He could elect to indulge in this easy source of detachment and try for intensity from a vivid dramatic characterization. Should he austerely invite further disadvantage by creating only anonymous characters, he might then concentrate upon the depiction of an exquisitely poised narrator, a civilized mediator between conflicting claims. A modern abstractionist is nothing if not ambitious. The subtle refinement upon esthetic disadvantage and abnegation can be carried still further in the creation of a merely neutral, uninvolved narrator. Then what would be left to exploit is an intellectualized excitement arising from a pure and memorable use of language and from a dazzling technique. This severe delimitation of the sources of empathy is a form of heroic endeavor; for, if the technique, metaphor, and language do not dazzle, the poet may end only as a juggler of formal devices or as an emotional eunuch—the common parodies of the Classicist in art.

The best of Ransom's poems about death are triumphs of consummately poised narration. In the poems about love Ransom is not as ingenious in his use of narrators; sometimes these figures are so superfluous that their mere appearance calls attention to Ransom's effort to control the tone and to make difficult transitions. But the successful poems about love reveal other ingenuities in poetic technique.

A group of four poems that deal with love and honor will illustrate Ransom's bewildering modernist attempt to refine upon impersonality and indirection: "Spectral Lovers," "Parting at

Dawn," "Parting, Without a Sequel," and "The Equilibrists."

I *Ironic Chill*

"Spectral Lovers" is a detached and ironical portrait of two anonymous people who respond to the enticements of an April night with appropriate feelings of eroticism but who succumb to the restraints of honor and timidity, and deny their bodies as effectually and completely as they would if they were spiritual beings purely:

> By night they haunted a thicket of April mist,
> Out of that black ground suddenly come to birth,
> Else angels lost in each other and fallen on earth.
> Lovers they knew they were, but why unclasped, unkissed?
> Why should two lovers go frozen apart in fear?
> And yet they were, they were.

The opening line creates atmosphere for the phantom relationship between the two people. "Haunted" is preparation for the idea that the lovers must have a spiritual genesis—holy or demonic, that they are not corporeal. Two polar possibilities—their materialization from the "black ground" or their misplacement as angels on earth—give the first hint of their besetting trouble. The poem begins very well, with a striking economy. Details that create atmosphere also prefigure the theme: these lovers appear spectral because they are walking in the mist and, more importantly, because they do not behave as lovers, for they "go frozen apart in fear."

Ransom has an excellent parody of a proper lovers' ritual in the tame "shredding of an April blossom." There is a coyness in the girl about this activity; though it is an implausible and tepid distraction, she hopes it will evoke a sexual response from her companion:

> Over the shredding of an April blossom
> Scarcely her fingers touched him, quick with care,
> Yet of evasions even she made a snare.
> The heart was bold that clanged within her bosom,
> The moment perfect, the time stopped for them,
> Still her face turned from him.

There is a disparity between her manner and her emotional

state, an equivocalness that contributes to the timidity of the man. She is ready to risk everything, to "surrender all," yet she falters: "Still her face turned from him." The strength of her passion and of her romantic mood is captured by vigorous and original images: "The heart was bold that clanged within her bosom"; "Strong were the batteries of the April night/And the stealthy emanations of the field." "Clanged" is a superb word for indirectly conveying powerful emotion. Strong "batteries" is a complex trope, suggesting both stored up electrical power for generating light (moonlight here) and an artillery barrage (a battering of the senses). A force parallel to the "mad moon" comes from the "stealthy emanations," the heady odors of foliage. But the woman remains passive, true to the convention of feminine modesty. The next set of allusions to chivalry is quite appropriate to the drama of this poem, but they are trite: "walls of her prison," "treasure," and "knight."

The paralysis of these lovers emerges. They both feel passion but do not act upon it because of a humane code of restraint. Two stanzas reveal the parallel dilemma of the man. His passionate exultancy is captured in his extravagant "gesturing" and in the bold projection of his mood upon the tall grass he is jauntily walking through: "swishing the jubilant grass." But this lyrical feeling has a counteraction; "considerations pinched his heart." "Pinched" gives a fresh illusion of concreteness and effectively renders his squeamishness. His sense of honor prevents him from releasing his strong, dammed-up passion (from reducing "his tributaries faster"). He feels a restraint that is quite incongruous to the art of love-making.

"Reeling with the sap of April" continues the ambitious indirection of presenting feelings through details of atmosphere:

> "Am I reeling with the sap of April like a drunkard?
> Blessed is he that taketh this richest of cities;
> But it is so stainless the sack were a thousand pities.
> This is that marble fortress not to be conquered,
> Lest its white peace in the black flame turn to tinder
> And an unutterable cinder."

Here Ransom begins to tax seriously our willingness to cooperate. Descent in zestful expression is abrupt in the return to the medieval-chivalric motif. The trite conceit of the citadel ("this richest of cities," "that marble fortress") glaringly reveals Ransom's determination to convey through objective data the man's chivalric inhibitions. The humorous exaggeration, the bombast, is too patent. We cannot attribute this archaic speech to a hyperformal young man; it becomes an intrusion by the author. "Lest its white peace in the black flame turn to tinder" is too literary. Erotic love between the man and woman is not even imaginatively credible when the speech becomes so artificial. Ransom continues the black and white imagery of the first stanza, but he does it so obtrusively and stiltedly that it is not a strength: "white peace in the black flame." "An unutterable cinder" sounds absurd, forced. In a poem so meticulously designed to avoid obviousness, this repeated implication that honor and chastity will be corrupted by lust is exorbitantly belabored.

The closing lines yield one more detail that combines atmosphere and theme: the spectral lovers are "White in the season's moon-gold and amethyst." This contrast between the rich colors of the environment and the bloodless pallor of ineffectual lovers is admirable, but the effect is suddenly undermined by the obviously pathetic analogy of the last two lines:

> They passed me once in April, in the mist.
> No other season is it when one walks and discovers
> Two tall and wandering, like spectral lovers,
> White in the season's moon-gold and amethyst,
> Who touch their quick fingers fluttering like a bird
> Whose songs shall never be heard.

The last-minute importation of the narrator is gratuitous. He provides only a mechanical repetition of April, the mist, and the ironical dilemma of the lovers. His presence—so dramatically unjustified—only underscores the anticlimactic ending. He makes no illuminating refinement upon the lovers' plight, no brilliant attenuation of the irony.

The best achievement of the poem is the successful inducing of the characters' inward state through details of the environment. However, the limitation of this indirection is that no intensity is built up. Ransom's brilliant manipulations of syntax and metaphor are sporadic, not marshaled into a gathering pattern that arrives at a satisfying culmination. The Classical poet, intent upon keeping the reader from a sympathetic identification with the lovers, has done his work too well: irony cools the emotion. Then the speeches, probably meant to be comic, are so stilted that the characters do not seem authentic. Archaic patterns of speech turn out to be not functional but strangely incongruous, contributing to an esthetic distance that is already too thorough. When the characters are portrayed with so little individuality, when their motives are treated so thinly and vaguely, and when the emotion is so remote, little potentiality for excitement is left except that which a sustained technical virtuosity can produce. The disjunct verbal excellences and the resourceful rhyming of this poem are not enough to distract the reader's attention from its lack of form and force.

"Parting at Dawn" and "Parting, Without a Sequel" have the same important defects but even fewer strengths. "Parting at Dawn," a glib and facile 'manufactured' poem about love and honor, has a paralyzing esthetic distance and a shifting, irresponsible irony. No feeling for the characters is allowed; the lovers are referred to as "them," and nowhere in the poem do they receive a greater particularity; they are more anonymous than the people in "Spectral Lovers."

In the first three lines a norm of strenuous self-denial is assumed: "If there was a broken whispering by night/It was an image of the coward heart,/But the white dawn assures them how to part. . . ." Night is conducive to love and therefore inimical to philosophical control and self-denial. "A broken whispering" of love betokens a weakness, a cowardly lapse from the norm of honor based upon austerity. The next two lines reinforce this norm; for, with the return of dawn, the lovers get back their correct perspective upon passion. "White dawn," "Stoics," "cold" light, and "the morning star" are closely related antitheses to romantic love.

Now the lovers are addressed by an anonymous person indistinct from the author: "Say then your parting; and most dry should you drain/Your lips of their wine, your eyes of the frantic rain,/Till these be as the barren cenobite." Presumably the effect Ransom seeks here is an intensification of the inward struggle by the poising of sexual innuendo, "wine" and "frantic rain," against extreme austerity, lips and eyes drained "most dry" and "barren cenobite." The very formal and rhetorical address, however, keeps the reader from any urgent feeling about the struggle.

The norm of honorable austerity predominates in the octave of this sonnet. If we have taken the norm seriously, though, we are about to be confused; for, in the sestet, the activities of the lovers who renounce their erotic and emotional impulses are treated with a casually skeptical tone. Our narrator—very sophisticated and arch, condescending and cynical—continues to address the unhearing lovers. The man is directed to embark upon a chivalric career of "wars and wounds," but he is described as "stumbling," which may suggest that he is pretentious in his ambition to fulfill his destiny according to austerity and heroics. To "Beat the air" until conscious of wasted time—the imperative given to the woman—does not seem to be a plausible and legitimate alternative to a life of love. Ransom is trifling with us and with his ideas.

The poem has another ironic turn to take. If the lovers who have renounced emotion should discover, ten years later, that their aborted emotional relationship still seems authentic and important, then they may conclude that they were wrong about the idealism that led them to self-denial: "Philosophy was wrong."

What a thin little imaginative artifact this poem is! As though the phantom characters did not thoroughly exclude any possible sympathy with their plight, Ransom contracts with an anonymous narrator to address them in an absurdly formal and stylized way ("if no Lethe flows beneath your casement") and to announce that there is no hope in either of the choices that young people have. They may succumb to a possibly shallow emotional relationship, or they may impose a restraint upon themselves that might prove to be pointless. Philosophy may be wrong, but they can learn that it is only by expending precious time in the service of illusory values and by foregoing pleasures that can be savored best in youth, present mirth that cannot be recaptured or redeemed later.

The tone of this poem is unpleasant; there is a smugness about the possible, or probable, futility of human existence and human values. It is a dishonest playing with irony; if that statement seems too strong, it is an irresponsible toying with ideas and values, like that in some of Stephen Crane's poems—a brittle, easily won coyness that likes to poise idealism against cynicism and stand back, noncommittally. All the esthetic decorum in

"Parting at Dawn" is uncalled-for, since Ransom has created no passionate life to impose it upon. There is nothing to carry the poem, no sustained verbal ingenuity, no subtle extension of idea.

Again, in "Parting, Without a Sequel" an assumed irony freezes out any possible feeling. The trick seems to be to present a character who has conflicting emotions, conflicting interests, and to assume that they cannot be resolved. Awareness of this frequent human difficulty would usually call for a response of pathos in the reader. Maybe Ransom hopes for one kind of anti-Victorian freshness in the mere withholding of a sympathetic response, in a serenely uncommitted, dispassionate portrayal of the forlorn character. Both the title and the emotional posture of the author are very stiff.

Projection of the woman's anger upon the words she writes is the best stroke in the opening lines:

> She has finished and sealed the letter
> At last, which he so richly has deserved,
> With characters venomous and hatefully curved,
> And nothing could be better.

Here is a successful example of Ransom's delicate method of indirection. "With characters venomous and hatefully curved" nicely suggests the feelings of the woman as she wrote. This device does not work as well, however, in the second stanza, with the riddling circumlocution—"blue-capped functioner of doom." Ransom wants an effect like that in "Dead Boy" when the coffin is described as "box of death"—something momentous is given a quick ironic association with something mundane. But here the absurdly comic overtones create too much emotional distance and the woman's solemn anxiety is lost. The self-conscious poet obtrudes when a Western Union boy is so clumsily and bombastically described. We infer the emotional state of the woman, her sense that this precise moment will gravely affect her future; but the 'literary' exaggeration provides too much insulation for us to take her feelings seriously.

The woman's emotional state is conveyed by precise physical description in the third stanza: fright mingles with anger and regret. "Too pale for tears" is an excellent psychological distinction for showing the disinclination to weep when fear predominates over regret; but Ransom tells obviously and directly what the woman has to fear: "the ruin of her younger years."

Now Ransom returns to the technique of projection, but not successfully. The "vaunting oak" (one of Ransom's favorite enigmatic phrases) is a contrivance, a stage effect; and the strange and memorable phrasing, "glistened/Stoical in the rain," only underscores the artificiality. A strained projection is supposed to justify the speech of the tree, this symbol of continuity with the past, this stable counselor:

> And now the agitation of the rain
> Rasped his sere leaves, and he talked low and gentle
> Reproaching the wan daughter by the lintel;
> Ceasing and beginning again.

We are far from an immediate sense of the woman's desperate plight when this bizarre substitute for a narrator begins to talk. "The wan daughter" is both repetitive and pompous.

The conclusion does not present a culminating revelation. It is merely a repetition of the irony of conflicting emotions that the second stanza makes all too explicit.

> Away went the messenger's bicycle,
> His serpent's track went up the hill forever,
> And all the time she stood there hot as fever
> And cold as any icicle.

"Serpent's track" is another effective projection of the woman's feeling upon a precise sense datum. The similes that conclude the poem—"hot as fever/And cold as any icicle"—are an unsatisfying repetition of the woman's paradoxical state, of her emotional muddle because she cannot reconcile the demands of love and personal honor. Ransom substitutes a weak and merely verbal climax for a thematic one. Personal pride leads her to an angry indignation; and, when she has acted upon this sense of honor, she is aware that she may have doomed herself to spinsterhood. It is impossible for the reader to judge whether her indignation is appropriate.

Ransom has presented a meager portrait of a woman who commits a hasty act that may have momentous consequences, but he has been content to repeat the woman's mixed feelings rather than to build up the opposing claims of those feelings so that some great tension might develop. Thinness of characterization and feebleness of thematic impact are not counterbalanced by resourceful metaphor or impressive language. The device of projection, even when not used erratically, is too slender to carry this poem; and Ransom's intuitive awareness that reinforcement is needed results only in a few gravely stilted phrases.

II *Audacious Technique*

The richest, the most fully developed, and the most technically resourceful of the love-versus-honor poems is "The Equilibrists." It is one of Ransom's most ambitious attempts to combine a mannered floridity with a tone of detachment; it is his most thorough triumph over his favorite self-imposed esthetic disadvantages. The poem begins with a rather intimate psychological revelation: presumably absent from his beloved, a man, whose consciousness is dominated by her appealing features, yearns for her lustfully.

> Full of her long white arms and milky skin
> He had a thousand times remembered sin.
> Alone in the press of people traveled he,
> Minding her jacinth, and myrrh, and ivory.

His preoccupation with her can give him a psychic isolation from a crowd of people. "Long white arms and milky skin" are subtle but strong erotic details. The emphasis upon arms is reminiscent of Prufrock's sedate and decorous erotic phantasy that shuns the grosser topography of breasts and thighs.

Ransom has begun a motif of embellishment that he will continue to use in the early stanzas. He follows up the explicit reference to "her long white arms and milky skin" with the metaphorical description, "her jacinth, and myrrh, and ivory"—an ornate use of metaphor, metaphor not as a startling economy and compression but as an embellishment that comes as anticlimax, as a leisurely imaginative afterthought to the denotation. It is a highly formal indirection, a covert way of keeping the reader detached from the characters.

This motif appears twice in the next stanza, after a witty epithet is used as an embellishment:

> Mouth he remembered: the quaint orifice
> From which came heat that flamed upon the kiss,
> Till cold words came down spiral from the head.
> Grey doves from the officious tower illsped.

"Quaint orifice," with its double innuendoes, could be written only by a poet who had savored his Donne. In the line "Till cold words came down spiral from the head," "words" and "head" are heightened by "cold" and "spiral"; but the line is merely denotative. It is followed by metaphors, "Grey doves" and "officious tower." "Grey" is excellent, implying not fresh and vigorous with passion, yet not splendidly innocent, either, but squeamish, uneasy. Ransom has now established the familiar counteraction to passion. The woman enticed the man, but repelled any sexual advance by her verbal waspishness. Her head, or intellect—"the officious tower"—sent out remonstrances against erotic action.

The motif of embellishment, resembling a comic parody of oratorical or legalistic definition, is continued in the naming of the body (rhetorically parallel to mouth, with "he remembered" implicit) and the addition of the metaphor, "a white field ready for love":

> Body: it was a white field ready for love,
> On her body's field, with the gaunt tower above,
> The lilies grew, beseeching him to take,
> If he would pluck and wear them, bruise and break.

The two conceits of tower and field are brought together here and the disharmony between body and head is elaborated. Her body was a field on which lilies grew, lilies that invited him to "pluck and wear them" (make use of in some way), "bruise and break"; but the "gaunt tower" was always ominously, forbiddingly there. Her body has a delicate beauty like that of lilies, yet the lust inherent in a body implies a paradoxical violence, a rude plucking of the fragile flowers.

> Eyes talking: Never mind the cruel words,
> Embrace my flowers, but not embrace the swords.
> But what they said, the doves came straightway flying
> And unsaid: Honor, Honor, they came crying.

The eyes 'speak' on behalf of eroticism. They say, "Never mind the cruel words" that come from the officious tower. "Flowers" and "swords" brought into sudden relation with "Embrace" is a startling extension of the image of lilies with sharp leaves. These eyes reflect a complicated awareness of the joy and danger (an awareness that the body does not have), but they suggest that love may be engaged in without spiritual harm, that the dilemma of love and honor can be transcended or ignored.

So far Ransom has managed to harmonize his theme and method, to refrain from particularizing his characters but nevertheless to generate an interest in their difficulty by trusting his invention of intricately related metaphors. Now he sets to work to smuggle more overt distance-creating devices into the poem. He slyly begins to insinuate an anonymous narrator, or commentator, in the next stanza:

> Importunate her doves. Too pure, too wise,
> Clambering on his shoulder, saying, Arise,
> Leave me now, and never let us meet,
> Eternal distance now command thy feet.

This stanza is a liability on several counts. The appraising comment, "Importunate her doves," makes us aware of the narrator, diverts our attention from the lovers' desperate state, and diminishes the personal immediacy of the dilemma. The description of the doves—"Clambering on his shoulder, saying, Arise"—is a stylized, Poe-like way of rendering the man's sense of inhibition, a Gothic decoration, embellishment run wild. "Eternal distance now command thy feet" is 'literary' and stilted bombast.

In the first line of the next stanza, our attention must be given again to the pompous narrator rather than to the lovers:

> Predicament indeed, which thus discovers
> Honor among thieves, Honor between lovers.
> O such a little word is Honor, they feel!
> But the grey word is between them cold as steel.

However, the apposition of thieves and lovers is a fresh turn on an old truism, suddenly hinting that the fulfillment of love demands a theft from the strict conscience. And the last line is an excellent gathering in of color, texture, and temperature to enliven an abstraction. Grey doves communicate the grey word

"Honor" which is as effectual an impediment to erotic love as the cold and deadly sword in the bed of storied medieval lovers.

Now the conventionalized, anonymous, omniscient, and merely reportorial narrator overtly enters. I suppose Ransom uses this stage-prop narrator, this choric monologist, as an expedient transition to the more satisfying distance-creating device, the Donnean and Marvellian metaphysical image. The poem's best phrase, "torture of equilibrium," is embodied in this image that gives an exciting cosmic counterpart of the lovers' agonizing repose.

> And rigid as two painful stars, and twirled
> About the clustered night their prison world,
> They burned with fierce love always to come near,
> But honor beat them back and kept them clear.

The simile of stars is given fresh life by "painful." These precarious lovers are like a double star in their apparent unity but inevitable separation from each other; their sense of honor that keeps them apart is as immutable and strong as cosmological laws. This figure is good preparation for the look at the stern, final equipoise: the transcendental consequences of either submitting to love or adhering to honor.

First, however, Ransom must bring his pompous narrator into the foreground again:

> Ah, the strict lovers, they are ruined now!
> I cried in anger. But with puddled brow
> Devising for those gibbeted and brave
> Came I descanting: Man, what would you have?

The nice economical summation of the phrase, "the strict lovers," is undermined by the turgid flatness of "I cried in anger." The last three lines of this stanza, designed as a transition to the perspective of eternity, have such a heavy rhetorical attitudinizing that they count as a liability in the total economy of the poem. Embellishment becomes strained. Although the paradox and irony of the lovers' dilemma have been firmly lodged with the reader, Ransom emphasizes them again with "gibbeted and brave." Ponderous artificiality serves no function when the narrator exclaims "Ah"; alludes to his "puddled brow," his "Devising," his "descanting"; and finishes with a piece of Biblical rhetoric.

Though the next three stanzas constitute the "descanting" of the narrator, he fades away from our consciousness as the compelling matter of these lines absorbs our attention, as we feel the splendid congruity between the thought and the language. Ransom's idea of dramatizing the ultimate implications of sexuality and honor is a very good one; the poem can be plausibly and richly extended, the irony given greater intensity:

> For spin your period out, and draw your breath,
> A kinder saeculum begins with Death.
> Would you ascend to Heaven and bodiless dwell?
> Or take your bodies honorless to Hell?

"Spin" keeps alive the metaphysical image of the lovers as stars caught in unique trajectory, and at the same time it allows us to think of *people* caught in the exhausting whirl of time and change. "Draw your breath," though an irrelevant reminder of Hamlet's last speech, is a nice understated way of suggesting immortality. If the lovers continue to breathe (a metaphoric version of "to have an existence") after spinning their earthly, mortal period out, the alternatives will be salvation, with a purely spiritual existence, and damnation, with a carnal insatiability. The irony of "A kinder saeculum" is too patent, for the next two stanzas are designed to convey the horrid bleakness of either translation, to Heaven or to Hell.

These two stanzas, the true climax of the poem, contain its best lines. Their effect is not to give us a glib and abstract excursion into philosophy but, by dramatizing the standard versions of salvation and damnation, to enhance the horror of our earthly doom: the unmanageable dualism of fleshliness and virtue. Emphasis falls not upon a facile spirituality (or immateriality), but upon our familiar view of ourselves as corporeal creatures. First, the loss of flesh (even as a prerequisite for Heaven) is made to seem unutterably grim:

> In Heaven you have heard no marriage is,
> No white flesh tinder to your lecheries,
> Your male and female tissue sweetly shaped
> Sublimed away, and furious blood escaped.

This assertion is a very quiet but chilling way of conveying the
hideous thought that the loss of sexual differences will mean es-
sentially the loss of humanness. ("Sublimed away" has an extraordinary richness, with connotations of chemistry, alchemy, psychology, and theology.) Then the *retention* of flesh—with its
insatiable appetites—is made to seem equally abhorrent:

> Great lovers lie in Hell, the stubborn ones
> Infatuate of the flesh upon the bones;
> Stuprate, they rend each other when they kiss,
> The pieces kiss again, no end to this.

The tone is supremely appropriate. These transcendental alternatives deserve a grave, ornate expression. The language is elevated, even archaic at times; but it is concise and arresting, and
imparts a density to the meaning it serves. Heaven is given a
dreadful blandness, tepidness; and Hell is given a furious futility
—the vanity of human wishes carried out to intolerable extremes.
These implications lend a powerful intensification to the lovers'
earthly frustration.

After this appalling dramatization of the poem's central irony,
the narrator's falsetto-voiced "But still I watched them" is weak
and anticlimactic. Our return to an earthly perspective is appropriate; but this persistent narrator, like many of Ransom's,
carries a cane which he uses to prod us into noticing transitions.

The poem concludes with a reminder of the enormous price
that must be paid for a balance between the demands of the
time-bound body and the spirit-obsessed mind. The epitaph has
two good lines, fortunately the final two of the poem. Parallel
to the image of the equilibristic lovers as "two painful stars"
unable "to come near" is the image of the two corpses *"untouch-
ing in each other's sight."* This poem's ultimate implication is
that the precarious and torturous balance forced upon human
beings by their dualism may be *rewarded* only with death, and
that all their unavoidable anguish may be meaningless and futile.

Ransom implies, as Emily Dickinson often did, that in humanity's imperfect and ambiguous state the good and tonic traits
are alloyed with, indeed are achieved by, pain and frustration.
An equilibrium that is torturous may be better than none at all;
yet it may be a vanity that the passionate, honorless adventurers

are right in ignoring. This poem lets loose such cosmic irresolution that the reader can never encompass it all.

"The Equilibrists" is a rare magician's art, a heroic Classical poet's art: to produce an esthetic intensity from the most meager and bare materials, to renounce the aid of an empathy that a reader might feel for particularized characters, to cut across the emotion of love with irony, to set up everywhere the defenses against an easy pathos, to work with a spare and severe emotional landscape, to trust ultimately an excitement sprung from sheer intellectual casuistry, from metaphoric and linguistic versatility. The emotion of the poem is induced by the working out of the thought, by the embellishment of it, by the subtle extension of it, and by the dramatization of its bewildering ironies—all dependent upon delicate adjustments of tone. Though the poem has some lapses, some too-obvious manifestations of modernist principles, it stands as one of the finest examples of Ransom's scrupulous mode of poetry. It is one of the best monuments of this century's debt to the tradition of Donne, to a poetry of passionate intellectual agility and inspired technical audacity.

When the ambitious reliance upon technical audacity flags, Ransom produces thin little failures. "Two in August" is undermined by startling lapses into direct and overt, uninteresting statement. Its subject is estrangement from love, a lovers' quarrel, a subject that could elicit some emotional intensity; however, because the reader's attention to the cenobitic thinness of characterization and coolness of detachment is not diverted by a protean intellectualism through technical virtuosity, the poem degenerates into banality, vapidity, and pretentiousness.

The opening crisply introduces the wedded duelists:

> Two that could not have lived their single lives
> As can some husbands and wives
> Did something strange: they tensed their vocal cords
> And attacked each other with silences and words
> Like catapulted stones and arrowed knives.

These two were not capable of being casual and indifferent toward an incompatibility, of being cynically nonchalant; they had to reflect their disturbed emotions. "They tensed their vocal cords," the poem's best single effect, is what Ransom likes to hit upon: an objective description that conveys inward feelings, that generates in the reader a sense of the characters' emotional state. This statement swiftly creates the atmosphere for a lovers' quarrel, and the atmosphere is further enhanced by the vivid simile, "Like catapulted stones and arrowed knives," that captures the emotional force of "silences and words."

The next lines, however, abruptly relinquish tonal control:

> Dawn was not yet; night is for loving or sleeping,
> Sweet dreams or safekeeping;
> Yet he of the wide brows that were used to laurel
> And she, the famed for gentleness, must quarrel.
> Furious both of them, and scared, and weeping.

Here we find a formidable collection of lapses in tone: the sentimental, "night is for loving or sleeping,/Sweet dreams or safekeeping"; the pompous, "he of the wide brows that were used to laurel/And she, the famed for gentleness"; the flat, "Furious both of them, and scared, and weeping." It must have been a fruitless search for something to heighten this little quarrel that sanctioned the naïve and wordy euphemism for poet. Ransom seldom writes such unrelievedly bad lines.

Though the banality of the next stanza is less complete, the flatness is preserved in the first two lines and in the lamentable abstraction, "entities," in the third:

> How sleepers groan, twitch, wake to such a mood
> Is not well understood,
> Nor why two entities grown almost one
> Should rend and murder trying to get undone,
> With individual tigers in their blood.

"Trying to get undone" is an excellent ambiguity in this unpromising verbal environment. It may mean unmated, disunited, or it may imply a strange perverse compulsion to become confused and wretched by surrendering to the negative emotion. "With individual tigers in their blood" parallels the similes of the first stanza, a capturing of inward ferocity. However thoroughly this struggle between love and anger is established, the poem does not have a dramatic course to run. The ending provides no climax of drama, of characterization, or of irony.

Flat and zestless phraseology continues: "She in terror fled from the marriage chamber"; "And he must tread barefooted the dim lawn,/Soon he was up and gone"; "Whether those bird-cries were of heaven or hell/There is no way to tell." The woman's nervous progress is described indistinctly, "like a string of amber." Whether amber is the color of the woman's hair or not, this is a strange and blurred simile, not connotative. "And would not light one lamp against the black" lamely works in cooperation with "trying to get undone." Although the literal meaning is plausible, the figurative meaning seems forced: she would not abate her anger, to conquer the black, negative mood. "Night-mastered birds" is a continuation of this imagery; the adjective is an obtuse reminder of the people who have been mastered by a negative emotion. "The long ditch of darkness" is not an attenuation of this motif but only a tiresome repetition of it.

I think this inconclusive ending reflects an esthetic desperation. Projection of the man's mood upon the birds is acceptable as an incidental effect, but *three* references to the bird cries constitute a default of theme and characterization and a surrender to atmosphere, to facile projection, as a way of wresting a climax from these obdurate materials.

Ransom has stoically denied himself the use of an anonymous narrator here and has sought to keep the anonymous characters before the reader very tenuously—allusively and elusively. He has tried to convey a mood that perversely acquiesces in a negative, destructive emotion, to imply that these people mysteriously deny themselves the healthy good will and light and lyricism of love. But he is not ingeniously and consistently indirect in this poem; he does not manage the tone; he erratically diverges in method between flat denotative statement and fanciful indirection. Parallel repetitious metaphors are an inadequate substitute for a culminating development. There is no resonance and grandeur of language to compensate for the poem's meager power to arouse empathy.

III *When Feeling Is First*

Besides "The Equilibrists," the only two poems about love that are positive successes are "Good Ships" and "Winter Remembered." Although they do not have individualized character-izations that quickly invite empathy, they benefit from a slight relenting in the rigorous assumption of disadvantages—an un-qualified commitment to the emotion of love. In "Good Ships" the commitment is implicit in the disparagement of a man and woman who meet for the first time but do not boldly respond to each other. This poem, a sonnet, has a convergence of theme and metaphor that permits Ransom to generate feeling yet pre-serve his scrupulous indirection and tone. The best single tech-nical attribute of the poem is the brave conceit of ships and sailing. This sustained metaphor enables Ransom to imply cer-tain strong qualities in his people and to invoke a healthy, posi-tive irony at the end; and it provides a suspensefulness about whether the parallel of ships and people can be sustained and whether it will yield a climactic turn at the end. Ransom displays a great versatility in drawing from the analogy different nuances of tone.

An exuberant, high-spirited tone attaches to "Fleet ships" and "high seas" and "unto the vast diverge." The people thus analo-gously described are capable of a magnificent self-reliance. Swiftly and compactly their attractiveness and grace are connoted in the splendid word, "Fleet." The phrase, "poised on the loud surge," inherits this tone and then is transfigured retroactively by the witty allusion to the place of the meeting: "one of Mrs. Grundy's Tuesday teas." With one astonishing economical stroke, Ransom establishes the atmosphere. Two people with rare human quali-ties meet in the dubious environment of a sickly conventional tea. "Loud surge" makes the talk amusingly palpable. "Poised" is an excellent pivotal word. It looks back to the positive conno-tations of the first two lines, but moves into the humorous impli-cation of trying to keep emotional balance among prudes and phonies.

Ransom now has the complexity of tone that he will preserve throughout the rest of the poem. We are thus prepared for the less than exemplary behavior of the man and woman. "Nor trimmed one sail to baffle the driving breeze" has a rare, excit-ing indirection. It reminds us again of the ships that can heartily navigate a great ocean; but the predominant idea, colored by the setting of Mrs. Grundy's house, is that the couple do nothing counter to the prevailing values. "Driving breeze" is a continuation of the humor in "loud surge," permitting Ransom to imply serious things in a comic way. We infer that the "good ships" submit to the force of the queasy environment; and this hint is followed up by the next line, a quick Prufrockian effect: "A macaroon absorbed all her emotion." The concise description of the man extends the analogy and may foreshadow the disparagement of the couple at the conclusion: "His hue was ashy but an effect of ocean." Dizzied by the noise of the crowd, becoming seasick, he is losing his balance. "But an effect of ocean" may imply that he registers only an effect of motion, whereas a more appropriate response to this meeting with an unusual woman would be an effect of *emotion*. The analogy is extended very deftly in the last line of the octave: "They exchanged the nautical technicalities." They made the conventional small talk expected of Mrs. Grundy's guests, but did not venture faithfully beyond.

"It was only a nothing or so" is an infelicitous repetition of what is skillfully, metaphorically, implied in "nautical technicalities." "Most certainly bound for port" is excellently rich in its double and paradoxical meanings of self-reliant control and meager investment in new and bold experiences. The people who could be fleet ships (who appear "So seaworthy one felt they could not sink") do not trust uncertainty and improvisation enough; they will not turn off the regular course for adventure's sake. They are not entirely complacent about the excessive planning and regularity, however, for "there was a tremor shook them." They are aware of what they might be missing by their guarded conventionality and decorous security. "Tremor shook them" is another admirable paradox: "shook" is appropriately applied to a sturdy ship; "tremor," to a delicate human emotional response.

Because of Ransom's extraordinary control of the analogy, the poem has an impressive ending. Without the slightest lapse in tone Ransom can write "Beautiful timbers" and suggest that the people are beautiful. The whole line, "Beautiful timbers fit for storm and sport," recaptures the exuberant capacity attributed to the couple at the beginning of the poem and adds, in a high-spirited figure, that these people have resources for engaging trouble as well as joy—"storm and sport." The concluding line is a culmination of the metaphorical motif, and of the paradox of strength and beauty undermined by timidity, and of Ransom's unfavorable judgment of people who have a lyrical adequacy for life but betray it. "Miserly" suggests paltry husbanding of emotion; "merchant hulks" swiftly transfigures the sportive fleet ships.

This poem is an admirable realization of Ransom's method. Scrupulously faithful to that method, he is seldom able to manage so rich a convergence of metaphorical ingenuity, theme, humor, value, irony, and anonymous characterization. Some of the power of "Good Ships" results from the abatement of esthetic asceticism, from the implicit commitment to the emotion dealt with. Ransom's assumption that the fulfillment of love is possible and right gives this poem a rare freedom from the sickly irony of impotence.

"Winter Remembered" is an even greater triumph of harmonious theme and method. Its technical strategy is an indirection managed by attaching a man's responses to weather and his feelings of emotional privation. The poem immediately finds its correct pitch, a balance between formality of language and precision of meaning:

> Two evils, monstrous either one apart,
> Possessed me, and were long and loath at going:
> A cry of Absence, Absence, in the heart,
> And in the wood the furious winter blowing.

Except for "long and loath," the rhetoric is not merely bloated language. When rhetorical heightening works in cooperation with precise meaning and pleasurable verbal effects, when elusive feeling is captured by striking phraseology, when a compression is achieved, our strict attention to the rhetoric is mitigated and we do not find it obtrusive; it quietly creates esthetic distance here. The rhetorical parallelism generates a suspense about whether the two evils are equally distressing. Two evils—each of which is monstrous when experienced separately, "apart" from the other—are presented vividly. "A cry of Absence, Absence, in the heart" conveys the relentless feeling of loneliness. Even the capital "A" increases the imperativeness and gravity of the mood. "The furious winter blowing" gives a simultaneity to snow, cold, and wind. "Furious" and "blowing" impart to the abstraction "winter" a fresh illusion of concreteness.

The second stanza begins the subordination of one evil to the other:

> Think not, when fire was bright upon my bricks,
> And past the tight boards hardly a wind could enter,
> I glowed like them, the simple burning sticks,
> Far from my cause, my proper heat and center.

Winter and Absence are not simply parallel oppressions. The rhetorical formality of "Think not" is quickly cut across by the brilliant and precise images of warmth and snugness: "when fire was bright upon my bricks,/And past the tight boards hardly a wind could enter." Mere counteraction to cold weather is gravely insufficient. Ransom now uses contrast to enhance the obsessive loneliness. Images of physical warmth, the fire bright upon the bricks and the "simple burning sticks," are cold comfort to one deprived of his beloved, his "proper heat and center."

The acute inadequacy and irrelevancy of physical comfort are quickly extended by images of cold. Because a warm fire is an ironic reminder of the essential internal warmth that is lacking, it would be better to endure "the frozen air." The logic of the second stanza is extended, attenuated, by outrageous paradox: healing induced by a deliberate exposure to the cold weather. When the beloved is absent, a numbness can be induced. The emotionally irrelevant weather could yield some relief in a numbness that would lower human consciousness and thus reduce the susceptibility to the pain of emotional deprivation. "Frozen air" is like "furious winter blowing" in its startling concreteness.

> And where I walked, the murderous winter blast
> Would have this body bowed, these eyeballs streaming,
> And though I think this heart's blood froze not fast
> It ran too small to spare one drop for dreaming.

As the poem nears its climax, the tone of detachment is covertly and variously protected. Emotional destitution is intensified by appalling images of bodily humiliation. This is hyperbolic asceticism contrived by quiet, precise, and straightforward description: "body bowed," "eyeballs streaming." The stark physiological nomenclature "eyeballs" is a foreshadowing of the naturalistic image that will conclude the poem. "It ran too small to spare one drop for dreaming," with its movement between blood and imagination, continues the bold concreteness. A fine casuistical distinction is made with "this heart's blood froze not fast"—a sheer minimal existence without enough margin to permit any feeling that is specifically human. This frigid asceticism is excellent preparation for the final stanza, which the reader awaits wondering what Ransom can possibly do to enhance the insensibility so far evoked.

This stanza ranks with Ransom's most excellent poetry:

> Dear love, these fingers that had known your touch,
> And tied our separate forces first together,
> Were ten poor idiot fingers not worth much,
> Ten frozen parsnips hanging in the weather.

The conventional address, "Dear love," preserves the formality and leads into the climactic synecdoche. Fingers that could transmit and register emotion when the lovers were together become "idiot fingers"—severely apathetic agents—when the lovers are separated. "Ten frozen parsnips hanging in the weather" is a subtle and shocking refinement upon the insensibility of "idiot fingers"; this is a grotesquely humorous and surrealistic evocation of emotional privation; it leaves the reader with an original and memorable sense of loneliness.

This concluding image centripetally pulls in all the motifs of the poem: the atmosphere of cold weather, the hyperbolic metaphor of psychic numbness induced by gradual exposure to the cold, the theme of loneliness, the consistently indirect celebration of the absent lover. The line fuses the two evils that the poem began with and dramatizes the marvelous transmutation that has taken place as one evil—cold weather—has become both the atmosphere for the poem and the agent of the induced numbness that is paradoxically the only source of relief for the evil of loneliness. The line has a ring of completeness in the reduction of a whole emotional being to a frozen physiology.

"Winter Remembered" is Ransom's only vigorous love poem. Much of its strength derives from the unqualified commitment to the emotion. All the ingenuity of metaphor, the freshness of language, and the extension of hyperbole are subordinate to the attempt to praise a woman. The source of the poem's form is the pattern of indirection. First, winter and absence (outward and inward cold) are paralleled. Then outward cold is deftly made to subserve inward cold; here begins a theme of love as the central meaning and motive of a human life. Images that suggest physical warmth have a bleakness when compared with the authentic inward heat that can be generated only by love. With brilliant casuistry, this logic is extended. So inefficacious is physical warmth, so far is it from satisfying the essential need of the person deprived of love, that it is better to reject utterly its false, superficial comfort, which is at best a bitter ironic reminder of inward privation, and to invite a deliberate bodily numbness. The climactic ending, "Ten frozen parsnips hanging in the weather"—a stark naturalistic image—is both thematically and technically the culmination of a lyrical purpose, the celebration of love. Few of Ransom's poems arrive at this superb integration of emotional power and modernist tone and indirection.

Ransom's self-consciousness about his modernism leads him into daring experimentation with emotional meagerness. Reflected in these poems about love are the healthy first principles of an artist: do something new; do something extraordinary. Conventional poetry about love follows the easy routes: it assumes that outward Nature is the harmonious ally of inward feeling; provides embellishment by lush, sensuous description of interiors; uses emotional overstatement, the grandiose adjective. In scorning these transparent devices and in concentrating on formal audacity, Ransom becomes like his equilibrists, caught between a poet's necessity to deal with emotion and a self-conscious modernist's preoccupation with subtle technical execution.

His major weakness seems to be that he often settles for a sophisticated execution without emotional power or the clear lyric line: he frequently incurs more disadvantages than he can transcend through a strict fidelity to his principles. His impotent poems about love are skeletal reflections of his fatal obsession with technique. Sometimes his poetry seems like a deliberate, narcissistic cerebral amusement rather than an adventure in the brave encompassing of life. Only in "The Equilibrists," a flawed masterpiece, does he extract an overwhelming passion from his uncompromisingly meager poetics. But the devices sometimes announce themselves, and the passion is intellectual; it is not an esthetic *ecstasy*. To achieve that, he has to permit feeling to be first.

In "Winter Remembered" all of Ransom's *important* principles are not only intact, but they are amenable to an unobtrusive sophisticated power. The very indirection is a source of excitement when it works so quietly to unleash emotion. Our awe at discovering that the emotion of love can be intensified by the bizarre image of frozen parsnips is the best authentication of Ransom's singular control. This reclamation of unpoetic resources is the highest pitch of Ransom's monastic ecstasy.

CHAPTER 4

Gravity and Grandiloquence:
The Poems about Time and Change

THE SUBJECT of time should be a felicitous one for Ransom, adapted to his esthetic predilections: his pleasure in circumventing standard responses and achieving the just and appropriate tone, his love of a grave sonority, his desire to practice his decorum and irony. Nostalgia is one of the perilous invitations to emotional intemperance. Changefulness can elicit either self-pity over the sad decline of all things or the counterdistortion, shrill exuberance over the inspiriting whirl and variety—elation based upon a partial view, with a convenient omission of the harsh decline and deterioration that time exacts.

Strangely, however, this group of poems has little variety in bold technical experimentation. There are no judiciously poised narrators as in the excellent poems about death; there is no sustained metaphorical dazzle as in the excellent poems about love. There are no memorable characterizations, no bewildering attenuations of irony. Whatever boldness these poems have lies in their almost exclusive dependence upon sheer language for subtle control of tone. This technique would be perilous enough for any poet; but, with Ransom's susceptibility to verbal archaism and to grandiloquence, it is a flirtation with disaster.

I *The Double Peril of Sentimentality*

Our familiarity with Ransom's principled efforts to avoid naïveté engenders a fresh curiosity about the very title, "Old Man Playing with Children." How can he manage a poem that has so simple a fiction and so disarming an esthetic guilelessness as the opening lines portend?

> A discreet householder exclaims on the grandsire
> In warpaint and feathers, with fierce grandsons and axes
> Dancing round a backyard fire of boxes:
> "Watch grandfather, he'll set the house on fire."

This pompous diction—"A discreet householder," "exclaims on," and "grandsire"—clashes with the prosy, laborious directness of the three lines that follow. The heavy word "discreet" gives the whole poem away at the beginning and coerces the reader into a crude antipathy for the "householder." Strain and ineptitude that begin the poem go unrelieved as the narrator announces himself:

> But I will unriddle for you the thought of his mind,
> An old one you cannot open with conversation.
> What animates the thin legs in risky motion?
> Mixes the snow on the head with snow on the wind?

This stance is an extraordinary one for Ransom to take: he commits himself unqualifiedly and unironically to the old man's participation in the games of children. It is a naïve idea that could be redeemed only by a great ingenuity of presentation; instead, the crude device of the omniscient narrator is used. This narrator has a purely mechanical function, to relay to the reader the old man's thought; his presence is not justified by a more subtle or more complex view than the old man's. Unusual language is intended to heighten this frail little conception, but much of it is bombast that only underscores the meagerness. "Unriddle" is a pretentious word for so simple a thought as the one that follows. The reticence of the "old one" is insisted upon as a specious excuse for the intervention of the narrator and as a sentimental appeal for the reader's sympathy with the grandfather. An attempt at economical description, "What animates the thin legs in risky motion?" results in abstract verbiage. The wintry metaphysical image—"Mixes the snow on the head with snow on the wind"—by exaggerating recklessness, undermines the defense of the old man's folly.

This analogy of the white hair of old age and the wildness of nature introduces too predictably the grandfather's denunciation of a tame conventionality and his flat and implausible assertion, "This life is not good but in danger and in joy." The interpolated speech of the grandfather contains sporadic strength of diction, but the uneven style continues—the oscillation between un-heightened, obvious denotation and stilted overstatement:

> "Grandson, grandsire. We are equally boy and boy.
> Do not offer your reclining-chair and slippers
> With tedious old women talking in wrappers.
> This life is not good but in danger and in joy.
>
> "It is you the elder to these and younger to me
> Who are penned as slaves by properties and causes
> And never walk from your insupportable houses
> And shamefully, when boys shout, go in and flee.
>
> "May God forgive me, I know your middling ways,
> Having taken care and performed ignominies unreckoned
> Between the first brief childhood and the brief second,
> But I will be more honorable in these days."

Rarely does Ransom abandon his guards against naïveté and banality as he does in the bloated thematic line, "This life is not good but in danger and in joy." The pedantic precision of "the elder to these and younger to me" is comic and weakens the desired effect of an indignant denunciation. Outrage is made shrill and implausible, too, by the artificial phrasing: "penned as slaves by properties and causes," "go in and flee," "performed ignominies unreckoned."

Four words are arresting for positive reasons. "Reclining-chair" suggests one of the paltry alternatives to the old man's aberrant behavior: an invitation to collapse into senility and inactivity. "Insupportable" (literally, intolerable) connotes not breadwin-ning, but the inability of the children's parents to 'keep' a house with the proper genial human spirit. "Middling" sums up the object of the whole attack: tepidness and cautiousness in the middle-aged people, a joyless middle-of-the-road safety in fore-thought and prudence. "Honorable" sets up an ironical dispar-agement of the parents, suggesting that it is dishonorable to be self-consciously aloof from imaginative play and unsympathetic toward the poetry of life.

A minor favorable ingenuity is the slant rhyme of the middle lines that is sustained for four stanzas, but its abortive omission from the concluding stanza is a little unsatisfying.

Perhaps the little flashes of control have seemed enough to Ransom to persuade him to keep "Old Man Playing with Children" among his selected poems, but the flagrant deficiencies in the poised treatment that he values so highly render it an anomaly. It is a collection of misfirings: the banal and naïve theme is momentously overstated; the technique is uninspired; there is no fresh narrative perspective to transcend earnest prosiness. Instead of the tactfully heightened language that might have saved the work, Ransom produces a deal of stilted bombast.

"Old Man Playing with Children" shows Ransom implausibly succumbing to sentimentality. It is quite an unscrupulous performance. Much more appropriate to his conscientious principles are the flaws of "Conrad in Twilight" and "Vaunting Oak," flaws precipitated by a recoil from sentimentality, by elaborate, contorted efforts to avoid it. "Conrad in Twilight" is marred by an unevenness of execution and by a jarring inconsistency of tone. In these weaknesses it is like "Janet Waking" and "Here Lies a Lady." In the mockery of an old man and his infirmities, Ransom assumes a serenely humorous detachment:

> Conrad, Conrad, aren't you old
> To sit so late in your mouldy garden?
> And I think Conrad knows it well,
> Nursing his knees, too rheumy and cold
> To warm the wraith of a Forest of Arden.
>
> Neuralgia in the back of his neck,
> His lungs filling with such miasma,
> His feet dipping in leafage and muck:
> Conrad! you've forgotten asthma.

Rhetorical address, with the repetition of the name, gives this opening the lyric formality of a child's jingle, suggesting that Conrad is merely a fictional effigy, not to be taken seriously. After this insulating mood has been established, perhaps, we can take in, without feelings of pathos, the somber picture of a frail old man in an inhospitable environment. The pain and debility of old age *can* yield a comic effect when presented so lightly. But the phrase "wraith of a Forest of Arden"—a strained concession to rhyme—is an unfortunate fall from detachment into flippancy and whimsicality. Conrad's wish to be warmed and reinvigorated by nature is cruelly negated by the bizarre contrast of the "mouldy garden" with the "Forest of Arden." Ransom's determination to be tough about this inherently pathetic subject is too patent; it produces the pathological rehearsal of the second stanza with the kind of absurd objectivity that is found in the description of Janet's hen succumbing to the poison of the bee. At this point, the reader has a great curiosity about the plausible design of this poem. What is the purpose of this severity of comic detachment? It should be something more than shocking novelty of treatment.

Lighthearted presentation continues in the emphasis upon Conrad's superficial comforts, so inadequate to reduce his essential ail:

> Conrad's house has thick red walls,
> The log on Conrad's hearth is blazing,
> Slippers and pipe and tea are served,
> Butter and toast are meant for pleasing!
> Still Conrad's back is not uncurved
> And here's an autumn on him, teasing.

Militant unconventionality of treatment reaches its limit with the illogical "Still" of the fifth line. Ransom's attempt to extract humor from the fact that aging cannot be arrested by indoor comforts results in facile nonsense. A transition to the excellent conclusion is made with the double meaning of "here's an autumn on him," but the word "teasing" with its flippancy keeps this line from being an effective tonal modulation:

> Autumn days in our section
> Are the most used-up thing on earth
> (Or in the waters under the earth)
> Having no more color nor predilection
> Than cornstalks too wet for the fire,
> A ribbon rotting on the byre,
> A man's face as weathered as straw
> By the summer's flare and winter's flaw.

This part of the poem is quite disjunct in tone and method from the lines that precede it. Aging, with its decline and depletion, is not inherently a comic subject. Only by assuming a strained toughness of sensibility can a poet pretend that it is, and that distortion is as offensive as a sentimental treatment. Ransom arouses our interest in his eccentric whimsicality; and, as we watch for a consummation of it, he shifts the tone to a quiet somberness.

This stanza—so admirable by itself if it were not intended as the consummation of what precedes it—avoids sentimentality without undermining legitimate pathos. It is an unflagging engagement of mutability; but, in place of a facetious detachment, Ransom achieves an unobtrusive, appropriately grave tone. Language used to sketch the decline of the year has delicate overtones that make it applicable to the theme of Conrad's worn-outness. A bold personification of "autumn days" provides license for using the poem's best single word, "predilection," and thus initiating the effective pattern of objective details that imply the sad decline of a man. The dreadfulness of a person without predilection is quietly suggested: a sensibility fallen into desuetude. "A man's face" is a deft reminder of Conrad. It parallels the inert objects that have been weathered, the "cornstalks too wet for the fire," and "A ribbon rotting on the byre." "A man's face as weathered as straw" has a sharp understated chill.

The final line is admirable: it has a rhetorical balance not won at the expense of meaning, and it derives an unusual, slightly archaic flavor from the use of "flare" for sun and "flaw" for wind. These words have rich overtones under perfect control. "Summer's flare" implies the strong passions of human maturity; "winter's flaw" implies the 'flawed' time of the year when death predominates in nature, when the cold hastens imperfections in a human body. Theme and method are nicely fused as a human face and straw are syntactically related to the natural alternations of weather that contribute to their change.

The great distinction of this stanza is to rescue from obviousness the parallel between autumn and old age. Too late for the poem's integrity, Ransom discovers the proper tone for his subject and is able to abandon the mocking humor. He relies mainly on terse indirect statement: the strategy of discussing "autumn days" in order to evoke a restrained sadness in the aging and wearing out of a man; and on a heightening through unusual language: "predilection," "flare," and "flaw." Only "byre" seems a little quaint and forced. This admirable method generates very elusive feelings about time's steady and indiscriminate attrition. If the whole poem were of this quality, it would rank with Ransom's finest.

Inconsistency of tone mars "Vaunting Oak"; and the trouble lies with the alternations in the subtle effects produced by language, more fluctuations between an offensive, pedantic whimsicality and a subdued gravity. The unfortunate statement, "He is a tower unleaning," gives this poem a falseness from the start. "Unleaning" is supposed to be the most striking word in this line, but it has a negative value as a gratuitous, pretentious substitute for "straight." There is no purpose served by personifying the tree at this point; furthermore, to personify it and then immediately to call it "a tower" compounds the metaphorical strain and artificiality. This abortive metaphor is followed by a bantering tone, a jauntiness: "He is a tower unleaning. But how will he not break,/If Heaven assault him with full wind and sleet,/And what uproar tall trees concumbent make!"

Ransom is attempting something very subtle in these lines. He is depending upon a formal phraseology and a mannered pomposity of syntax to create esthetic distance. This technique requires a precarious balance between the subject and the tone lest the treatment degenerate into farce or ponderous whimsicality. Disparities, discrepancies announce themselves. When formal rhetoric is used in this jaunty spirit, it may become pedantic. "How will he not break," "If Heaven assault him," and "full wind and sleet" give the opening a heavy wordiness to go with the clumsy metaphor. "Concumbent" is bombastic when applied to a tree. These are creaks of a sluggish machinery for managing tone.

Then inversion and extravagant Latinate diction become conspicuous:

> More than a hundred years, more than a hundred feet
> Naked he rears against the cold skies eruptive;
> Only his temporal twigs are unsure of seat,
>
> And the frail leaves of a season, which are susceptive
> Of the mad humors of wind, and turn and flee
> In panic round the stem on which they are captive.

The impressive age and height of the tree do not justify the melodramatic description, "Naked he rears against the cold skies eruptive." "Naked" and "rears" parallel "concumbent" in bombast, and "cold skies eruptive" adds an obtrusive and awkward syntax to the florid language. "Temporal" and "seat" are pretentious and academic. The strictness of the *terza rima*, which could inspire a resourceful rhyming, in this poem only underscores the rigid effort of contrivance. "Eruptive" begets the *shrilly* Latinate "susceptive" and invites the melodramatic "captive." Even Ransom's adjectives are obvious, used to engender the strange mixture of pathos and arch humor: "cold skies," "temporal twigs," "frail leaves," "mad humors." Strained, pathetic expression undermines a vivid metamorphic image of the leaves.

This start is quite unpromising. Ransom chooses to control the tone through the greatly limited and difficult resource of diction. Stilted phrasing continues as the narrator emerges: the elaborate circumlocution for "me"—"an unbeliever of bitter blood"—sounds too archly self-effacing. The synecdoche for the girl, "a certain heart," is a curious mingling of abstraction with standard sentimentality. "Eminent witness of life" is pedantic. "The summer's brood" is dull poetic diction. The girl speaks as pompously as the narrator; the design of the poem calls for a sharp distinction of their personalities that speech should register.

One phrase comes up to the standard that Ransom presumably sought: "phantasy of good" is bold and original, and does not sink with heavy denotation but works on the reader with lingering overtones. It captures the girl's strong mood of optimism, her great hopefulness. And it has a lightly comic suggestion of a heady youthful exuberance, an immature optimism.

This subtle control is lost, however, in the sudden reversion to inflated language and inept metaphor as the leafing of the oak (already represented as "he") is analogized to childbearing: "Then the venerable oak, delivered of his pangs,/Put forth profuse his great banners of peace/And testified to her with innumerable tongues." The passage is offensive in its attempt to keep alive the halfhearted personification and in its substitution of sentimentality for a proper gentle gravity. "Green banners of peace" is execrable poetic diction for leaves. Incongruity runs wild: "green banners" do not suit well with either obstetrical 'delivery' or "tongues." This passage would rival Joyce Kilmer's achievement in incompatible metaphor.

Though tone, economy, and language perceptibly improve

from this point, the next section is plagued by an obscurity:

> And what but she fetch me up to the steep place
> Where the oak vaunted? A flat where birdsong flew
> Had to be traversed; and a quick populace
>
> Of daisies, and yellow kinds; and here she knew,
> Who had been instructed of much mortality,
> Better than brag in this distraught purlieu.

This expression is formal but not contrived and not self-consciously facetious. The "birdsong" is an important recurrence to the "summer's brood" of the fifth stanza, for it will figure in the poem's climax. The banal statement, "A flat where birdsong flew/Had to be traversed," contrasts with the splendidly somber phrase, "this distraught purlieu." Cleanth Brooks must assume that "this distraught purlieu" refers merely to the mortal, ephemeral lives of the birds and flowers that inhabit this flat (*Sewanee Review*, LVI, 407). In that reading, the phrase is another piece of bombast. It can be strongly justified, however, if something more than birds and flowers is being described. If this dramatic ephemeral life is found in the family graveyard, there is more point to the excellently solemn description of the girl, "instructed of much mortality": she has suffered the dying of some of her people. She has already said that the oak would be a better symbol of love's permanence than the "summer's brood," and the narrator is not tediously repeating that idea. A small graveyard with "dusty tombs" is another deep contrary evidence for her sanguine optimism to resist. Though the girl is "wrapped in a phantasy of good" and would like to make the phantasy prevail with her companion, she has misgivings. This complexity is important for her behavior at the end of the poem.

Isn't the graveyard *named* in the next line? "Above the little and their dusty tombs was he/Standing, sheer on his hill, not much soiled over/By the knobs and broken boughs of an old tree. . . ." These words create a vivid image of the tree high above the tombstones of frail and mortal people, and preserve suspensefully the possibility that something material is free from the dominion of time and change. A confusion enters here, however. This oak tree, which has been consistently personified throughout the poem, is said to be "Standing, sheer on his hill," and personification is thus continued; but, when "he" is said to be "not much soiled over/By the knobs and broken boughs of an old tree," we must wonder whether Ransom has committed a logical ineptitude for the sake of rhyme and has said that the tree has been not much defaced by the scars of an old tree (itself), or whether the "he" is an immaterial essence embodied in the tree. This confusion is inherent in the next lines: "And she murmured, 'Established, you see him there! forever.'/But, that her pitiful error be undone,/I knocked on his house loudly, a sorrowing lover. . . ." So the muddle is hopelessly complete. The tree cannot be both "him" and "his house."

Yet, late in the poem, as in "Conrad in Twilight," Ransom now implausibly gains an admirable control:

> And drew forth like a funeral a hollow tone.
> "The old gentleman," I grieved, "holds gallantly,
> But before our joy shall have lapsed, even, will be gone."
>
> I knocked more sternly, and his dolorous cry
> Boomed till its loud reverberance outsounded
> The singing of bees; or the coward birds that fly
>
> Otherwhere with their songs when summer is sped,
> And if they stayed would perish miserably;
> Or the tears of a girl remembering her dread.

"Like a funeral" is probably too transparent and cumbersome, but the rest is impressive. Ransom conveys the idea that change *shall* have dominion; he does it through the dramatic action of the narrator and the inspired contrast of sounds. The hollow sound of the tree when rapped upon, "his dolorous cry"—his cry of approaching death—is louder than any positive, living sounds: "The singing of bees" or birds, or the weeping of the girl, who realizes that her "phantasy of good" is an illusion. The way the girl is brought back to our attention is similar to the way Conrad is: each is mentioned as one of a series, and the importance of the character's re-entry is implied, not overstated. Quiet endings are appropriate to the somber theme, but they are not satisfying consummations of the florid whimsicality these poems begin with.

"Vaunting Oak" concludes with no inversions, no syntactical wrenching, no implausible archaisms. Important words and phrases have an unusual cast that gently enhances the grief.

There is no specious effort to mask the sadness by the narrator's extravagant speech. The narrator uses a temperate formality, language that subserves mood but does not shout eccentricity: "drew forth," "holds gallantly," "more sternly," "dolorous cry," "loud reverberance outsounded," "coward birds that fly/Otherwhere," "when summer is sped," "remembering her dread."

If, as Cleanth Brooks believes, all the turgidity of this poem is intended as a parody of the grand style, then the poem should find its resolution in this spirit and at least be unpretentious if bad. A sudden shift to sobriety in the conclusion will not evaporate from the reader's consciousness the contorted language he has lived through up to that point. Tone cannot be achieved separately from the characters and the theme. If we are assessing a poem's integrity, let us be as hesitant about thoughtlessly cooperating with Ransom's eccentric indirectness by whimsicality as with Shelley's pathetic directness.

These three poems show Ransom's attraction to the subject of time and to the perilously subtle management of the subject by a heightened language. "Old Man Playing with Children" is a quaint parody of Ransom's esthetic principles. "Conrad in Twilight" and "Vaunting Oak" offer sporadic hopeful intimations of what might be done, though they fail as wholes. They are ultimately sad poems, and the only plausible explanation for the elaborately jocose beginnings is that Ransom seeks to disarm the reader with a leisurely good humor, to avert the immediate stock response to the pathos of mutability, to practice a versatility in modulating to somberness at the end.

II *A Purer Language*

Two poems dealing with the horror of change have less cumbersome machinery for managing tone. The difference in quality between "Vision by Sweetwater" and "Blue Girls" is attributable mainly to language. Presumably Ransom has had some misgivings about "Vision by Sweetwater," for he omitted it from the 1945 edition of his *Selected Poems*. It may be his quietest poem on the subject of change. The charm comes from quick, bright images rather than resourcefulness of soberly ornate language. It has no intricate pattern of development, no characterization, no ingeniously poised method of narration, no striking metaphorical freshness. It is like many of Poe's poems in simplicity of technique and vagueness of point. In its delicate cadence there is a pure lyricism rare in modern poetry.

I think the effect Ransom seeks is a quick sense of the horror implicit in a fresh youthfulness threatened with perishability. The beginning evokes a lovely and delicate picture of the girls, not through a precise description but through an association of them with the local scenery:

> Go and ask Robin to bring the girls over
> To Sweetwater, said my Aunt; and that was why
> It was like a dream of ladies sweeping by
> The willows, clouds, deep meadowgrass, and the river.

The excellent conversational yet lyrical narration is marred by the standard inept narrative phrase, "and that was why," suggesting that Ransom is not interested in a consistently subtle presentation, or is more interested in rhyme. "Dream" is vague but relevant to the vision of the title and to the blurring of time—past, present, and future—that occurs throughout the poem. After the sudden evocation of the lovely, youthful girls in motion, Ransom uses sound to intensify their elusive charm and delicacy:

> Robin's sisters and my Aunt's lily daughter
> Laughed and talked, and tinkled light as wrens
> If there were a little colony all hens
> To go walking by the steep turn of Sweetwater.

"Lily," a deft mediatory word, continues the sense of the girls' fragile, bright loveliness and prepares for the soft and happy sounds they make. "Tinkled light as wrens" carries on the suggestion of dainty movement and adds delicacy of sound. The effect is quickly diminished, however, by the awkward line that follows it, a hair-splitting speculation: if there could be a colony of wrens that was entirely female—hen wrens. This quaint drollery has the effect of an author's intrusion. Wry casuistry breaks the precariously created lyric mood. It is unfortunate because the emphasis of the poem is upon the dreamlike quality of this experience, with its horrifying intimation of destructive aging:

Let them alone, dear Aunt, just for one minute
Till I go fishing in the dark of my mind:
Where have I seen before, against the wind,
These bright virgins, robed and bare of bonnet,

Flowing with music of their strange quick tongue
And adventuring with delicate paces by the stream,—
Myself a child, old suddenly at the scream
From one of the white throats which it hid among?

"Dark of my mind" is preparation for something grim—an equivalent of Frost's "desert places." The narrator is aware that these fresh, blooming girls, with their light steps and tinkling voices, are one of the appearances that recur in his dreamlike movement through time. He recalls an earlier experience like this one ("Myself a child") when a dissonant scream from one of the girls propelled him into the future and made him feel sharply his own subsequent aging. Was it a literal experience from his past or a 'racial memory,' something vaguely recalled from an old romance or from Classic or Medieval literature? The contrasting tones of "scream" and "white throats" make implicit the horror in a youthfulness that can perish.

This poem has a better structure than "Conrad in Twilight" and "Vaunting Oak," but again the turn toward the climactic ending is accomplished clumsily, pompously: "Let them alone, dear Aunt." "Vision by Sweetwater" has a few striking phrases: "tinkled light as wrens," "Flowing with music of their strange quick tongue" (a superb dreamlike effect in the assimilation of sound and movement). Ransom does not try for much richness and resonance here; he does not take many rhetorical chances. Perhaps that is why there are so few stilted and whimsical phrases: "fishing in the dark of my mind," "robed and bare of bonnet." "Vision by Sweetwater" has a strange insubstantiality. Its meager language cannot hide the impoverishment and keep the poem from paling in the reader's memory. The poem itself succumbs to mutability.

"Blue Girls" has no greater ambitiousness of metaphor or of characterization, but its linguistic boldness gives a solidity to the theme of mutability. A pleasing rhetorical elegance is apparent at the beginning:

> Twirling your blue skirts, travelling the sward
> Under the towers of your seminary,
> Go listen to your teachers old and contrary
> Without believing a word.

Rhetorical balance and alliterative parallelism in the first line create a formal distance without artificiality. The archaic "sward" has a subtle appropriateness to the seminary with its old teachers; it is not a variant of "lawn" that is used merely for whimsical ornamentation. It contributes to the atmosphere, a stodgy formality—in conflict with the bright, lyric youth of the girls. The blue and green and the twirling and traveling—with connotations of youthful freshness and liveliness—are played off against the heavy "towers of your seminary" and the "teachers old and contrary."

Much as in the second stanza of "Vision by Sweetwater" the girls are next compared to birds as a way of suggesting their lightness and lyricism:

> Tie the white fillets then about your hair
> And think no more of what will come to pass
> Than bluebirds that go walking on the grass
> And chattering on the air.

The colors of the first stanza (the skirts and the sward) are repeated with the "bluebirds that go walking on the grass"; and the irrelevance of academic studies is implied again in "chattering on the air": talking with gaiety but to no intellectual purpose. "Come to pass" is a minor lapse into triteness.

The richest single word of the poem is in this stanza:

> Practise your beauty, blue girls, before it fail;
> And I will cry with my loud lips and publish
> Beauty which all our power shall never establish,
> It is so frail.

"Practise" implies a full commitment, a devoted attention—like that of a good medical man. Since it would ordinarily be associated with some discipline, it is an ironic reminder of the subject matter that the old teachers would foist on the girls. Girls can best practice their beauty by investing in the present moment, by valuing their bloom more than anything else, by having as little anxiety over the future as bluebirds do.

It might be argued that the excellence of the conclusion justifies the explicit attention now given to the narrator—some modulation is necessary—but the odd statement, "I will cry with my
loud lips," has an obvious and shrill urgency that does not ac-
company the quiet imperative, "Practise your beauty, blue girls."
It is the poem's worst lapse into artificiality: to publicize beauty
by crying with "loud lips" sounds like a posturing. This kind of
poetic datum is effective only if the reader kindly agrees not
to think about it definitely.

A word that is an ironic counterpart to "Practise" yields nearly
as much fresh evocation in this context. "Establish" has some
rich implications for the ontology of beauty, for the tyrannical
evanescence of it that cannot be arrested. Although by some
mysterious paradox beauty can be practiced, it cannot be made
stable, for it is an essence undergoing imperceptible destruction
by time even while it owes its being to time.

The conclusion has a calm forcefulness. It is one of Ransom's
finest passages:

> For I could tell you a story which is true;
> I know a lady with a terrible tongue,
> Blear eyes fallen from blue,
> All her perfections tarnished—yet it is not long
> Since she was lovelier than any of you.

A sense of lost music is induced by the epithet, "lady with a
terrible tongue." Her voice conveys the drastic physical decline,
the disfigurement caused by a bitter disposition—her ruined
beauty. Her "terrible tongue" contrasts with the harmlessness of
"chattering on the air." Then the subdued line, "Blear eyes fallen
from blue," communicates much more chilling horror about
human mutability than the report of a scream hidden among
white throats. Combination of sound and meaning makes it a
haunting line: the pleasing auditory effect of the alliteration,
"blear" and "blue," is savagely counteracted by the sense, the
metamorphosis of eyes from girl's to crone's, and by the ruth-
lessness of a natural process conveyed simply by "fallen." This
splendid pitch is sustained with the next phrase, "All her perfections tarnished." Destroyed perfections, vanished perfections,
lost perfections—all seem less horrible than "tarnished" ones.
"Tarnished" is excellent for carrying on the implication of a

natural process that gradually diminishes purity of beauty. The ending refines upon the repugnant inevitability of change. This deteriorated, embittered lady once was more enticing than any of the blue girls; their lithe beauty is thus made the more precarious and sad.

III Bombast and the Grand Style

The most dramatic contrasting examples of Ransom's bold use of language for tonal control are his two excursions into nostalgia. "Old Mansion" is filled with affectations, esthetic miscarriages; "Antique Harvesters" is Ransom's most ambitious and effective poem about time and change. "Old Mansion" is marred immediately by a self-conscious, heavy humor that engenders a pretentious diction. Though the subject is ultimately serious, Ransom's contrived mode of detachment commits him to a false tone. The language in stanza after stanza is negatively conspicuous. Again, Ransom relies mainly on diction to carry the poem; and he needs a highly versatile and flexible language to accomplish his purpose here.

The theme should be congenial for him: the proposition that the American South has produced a native and original antiquity. It is a serious theme approached with elaborate indirection so that the sobriety is masked by a sprightliness of tone and a casualness of narration. Ransom's effort to make the narrator function as his droll intermediary leads to most of the ponderous flaws of the work. The weaknesses of the opening lines are the ones that pervade the whole poem: pomposity and turgidity alternate. Verbiage appears immediately:

> As an intruder I trudged with careful innocence
> To mask in decency a meddlesome stare,
> Passing the old house often on its eminence,
> Exhaling my foreign weed on its weighted air.

"Careful innocence" has a complexity, but its emphasis is blunted when preceded by "trudged with" and followed by "To mask in decency a meddlesome stare," heavy and turgid diction. Even the slightest details are presented with swollen language: the house is not on a hill but an "eminence"; a cigar is "foreign weed." At first, the reader may faithfully assume that Ransom has some dramatic reason for making his narrator so wordy and so stuffy, remembering that a pompous character is used to good thematic purpose in "Puncture."

The next lines hint at the theme and identify the narrator as a historian:

> Here age seemed newly imaged for the historian
> After his monstrous chateaux on the Loire,
> A beauty not for depicting by old vulgarian
> Reiterations which gentle readers abhor.

The paradox of a new antiquity ("age seemed newly imaged") is what attracts this man; the clichés of European history would have to be transcended in order to capture this specifically American kind of nostalgia. After two good lines there is a reversion to the pretentious complex phrasing, the misfired elegance of rhetoric which is really only clumsy articulation. "Old vulgarian/Reiterations" amounts to self-indulgence in quaintness. "Vulgarian" must be the most pretentious synonym for "common" in the language. But after this extension of verbiage comes the trite "gentle readers."

The next five stanzas yield only a glimmering control. A good passage occurs rarely; flatness and artificiality predominate. "Each time of seeing" is awkward. "I absorbed some other feature" is dull. "A house whose annals in no wise could be brief/ Nor ignoble" is pedantic and plodding. The tone and elevation that Ransom wanted in this poem appear in "it expired as sweetly as Nature,/With her tinge of oxidation on autumn leaf." This resourceful language evokes a subtle and elusive quality of the house and gently implies a somber dignity accruing through time.

Banality returns with "It was a Southern manor," flaccidity with "One need hardly imagine . . . ," strained and awkward humor with "sufficient state if its peacock *was* a pigeon." This line thickly suggests that a mere pigeon generates enough stateliness at this manor; no pampered peacock is needed for an ornamental curiosity. The following line gives the reason: although no royalty mingles hereabouts, Southern decorum has bred ritualized patterns and has preserved a serious view of existence. In this line alone does the language enhance the subject. Three to one is roughly the ratio of bad lines to good in this part of a poem that becomes steadily worse.

Not even one line relieves the prosiness of the next stanza. "Where the catafalque/Had carried their dead" is not memorable but at least it has the virtue of being unobtrusive. Had Ransom been able to keep more of his undistinguished lines from making a negative impression, the good ones might have seemed more telling. "Projected a note too charnel" is abstract; it reflects Ransom's effort of contrivance. So does "intricate stalk," a superfluous and vague description meant to convey atmosphere.

A specious verbal complexity substitutes for the thematically important Southern nostalgia that Ransom cannot name or evoke. Ornateness with precision is needed here, but in "Stability was the character" and "Decay was the tone" Ransom has achieved only thin circumlocution. Next comes a stilted and melodramatic introduction to a stilted speech.

The speech of "the watchful heart" is the most artificial narrative device of the poem. It is an insipid kind of esthetic distance that results from a narrator's *report* of a speech given by a heart, a heart that speaks with a pompous Biblical rhetorical style. This discourse is so bad that it sounds like a wooden and literal translation of poetry from some intractable language. After this desperate shift the poem loses any claim upon our imaginations, and stolidly grinds along its pedantic course, with no deftness of narration and with only appallingly meager spurts of linguistic charm. In the five concluding stanzas all the burden is thrown upon ingenious phraseology; Ransom abandons subtlety of narration, and metaphor, and evolution of character. But, instead of charm, the language produces only bombast and banality. It is a dull story told by a facetious pedant. All the elaborate preparation is made for this anticlimax: the historian asked if he could look at the house or if they would tell him some stories about it, and a servant relayed the mistress' refusal. Ransom tries to keep alive the Europe-America contrast with "wrapped concierge and imperturbable vassal" and "the lords or the peons." This motif is an *ignis fatuus*, though, for the poem does not convey the sense of a new antiquity that is tantalizingly begun in the second stanza. The narrator imagines the fate of the house: it would crumble before any historian ("annalist") inspected it. Its future ruins could be unearthed and 'fingered' by an archaeologist, someone who examines artifacts too late to capture the human spirit animating them.

There is some effort to make the ending sound like an ending. The theme of a new antiquity is abandoned, and a flaccid generalization about the pervasiveness of change rung in. The narrator's statement, "I saw myself in the token,/How loving from my foreign weed the feather curled," suggests that as the tobacco is changing into smoke and nothingness, so is the house, and so is he. All he has for his trouble is a more intense awareness of change to carry to some less evocative or enticing tableau.

"Old Mansion" is a strange and strained poem, arousing curiosity it doesn't intend to satisfy. Its chief value must be ironic, negative: we see what an achievement it is to write "Antique Harvesters" and to keep the language from sinking into perilous distortions.

"Antique Harvesters" is probably Ransom's best effort to carry a poem by sheer strength of rhetoric. It is surely his most ambitious poem about time. Though the technique is flawed, the tonal control is much firmer than in "Old Mansion": no smug and flippant narrator presides; whatever skepticism or flippancy appears is integrated dramatically. Archaisms are used to create a moving nostalgia and are not offensively pedantic. Sometimes the emphasis falls not upon single archaic words but upon unusual phrases. Sometimes the syntax creates a heightened and dignified effect, as in the first line:

> Tawny are the leaves turned but they still hold,
> And it is harvest; what shall this land produce?
> A meager hill of kernels, a runnel of juice;
> Declension looks from our land, it is old.
> Therefore let us assemble, dry, grey, spare,
> And mild as yellow air.

This tone is quite different from that of "Old Mansion." Accompanying the title, a parenthetical description of the scene hints at some kind of pageantry, of formal enactment: *"Of the Mississippi the bank sinister, and of the Ohio the bank sinister."* These rivers form the natural borders of the Southland. The old-fashioned "sinister" and its inverted position are preparation for a theme of the Southern past and for a formal treatment of it.

"Antique Harvesters" keeps an almost unflagging congruity of
theme and tone.

The very beginning has a rhetorical heightening that sounds
natural and produces a somberness of image and intonation.
Description is not merely decorative; the leaves have turned,
but it is too early for them to fall. This distinction places the
emphasis upon the harvest time. The question and answer continue the grave formality, with a faint suggestion of a litany;
and in the answer come hints of the leanness of the harvest, a
good justification for the somber tone. An intensification of meagerness is achieved by the precise naming of "kernels" after the
"meager hill." "Runnel" has a good old-fashioned agrarian flavor,
implies a modest production, and provides an aural parallelism
with "hill" and "kernels." "A runnel of juice" is an excellent
liquid counterpart to the "meager hill of kernels."

However, admirable as these effects are, they are only a
prelude. The mood of the region and of its loyalists rings in one
eloquent line, "Declension looks from our land, it is old." This
is Ransom's sterling tone. "Declension" has a noble gravity. It is
not remarkable for its eccentricity; it is not pedantic. This unusual word, when combined with a fresh construction, "looks
from," produces a sublimity rare in American poetry. The injunc-
tion, "Therefore let us assemble," too patently underscores the
formal ritual that is the poem's fictional basis; but in the final
two lines we see the full relevance of the autumnal theme in
the opening line.

Autumn is the season of the year, the season of the South's
history, the season of the men's lives. The adjectives, "dry, grey,
spare," are relevant to all three and so is "mild as yellow air," a
splendid indefinite simile that coalesces tactile and visual sensa-
tion and sadly implies both an inward maturity of the men and
a ripeness of Southern civilization. It is an extraordinary stanza,
rich yet unified, magniloquent yet economical.

The next lines are not as consistently excellent:

> "I hear the croak of a raven's funeral wing."
> The young men would be joying in the song
> Of passionate birds; their memories are not long.
> What is it thus rehearsed in sable? "Nothing."
> Trust not but the old endure, and shall be older
> Than the scornful beholder.

Unsymmetrical use of "croak" with "wing" enhances the mysterious incantatory effect of this speech. Ransom has admirably avoided the use of a narrator; the skeptical and dissonant statement is made by some younger men, or it is imputed to them by the old men. The following two lines explain this dramatic opposition: young men are not "mild as yellow air" and presumably do not see how the somber autumnal mood and ritual are relevant to them. But the expression is weak: in the use of "joying" Ransom strikes a note of preciosity, even effeminateness; and, in the use of "passionate birds," he settles for a weakened reiteration of the admirably wild " 'croak of a raven's funeral wing.' " This diction is studied and strained; and it does not set up pleasant lingering aftereffects. "Trust not but" is Ransom's too easy way of achieving a specious solemnity through a markedly dated and awkward locution. It introduces a passage that eloquently implies the connection between good faith and human durability, an idea that will be insisted upon at the end of the poem. "Rehearsed in sable" has the proper elevation of tone and the connotation of a decorous ritual. The reply to the question is nicely ambiguous: if the skeptical young men say "Nothing," they are discounting the importance of the ritual espoused by the old men. If the old men say "Nothing" in response to their own question ("What is it thus rehearsed in sable?"), they are denying that the activity is gloomy. Because each version is plausible, the ambiguity enriches the drama.

The same ambiguity also holds for the quotation in the next stanza:

> We pluck the spindling ears and gather the corn.
> One spot has special yield? "On this spot stood
> Heroes and drenched it with their only blood."
> And talk meets talk, as echoes from the horn
> Of the hunter—echoes are the old men's arts,
> Ample are the chambers of their hearts.

With "spindling ears" the theme of meagerness is carried on. Ransom now gets some fresh value from the ancient theory that heroes' blood produces fertile soil. Scornful young men could say so and ridicule their elders by a derisive rehearsal of what they take to be a tired old metaphor of patriotism. Old men could say so in support of their belief in the ennobling self-sacrifice of ancestors. Thus the Civil War is implicitly connected with the harvest ritual. Ritualism is subtly reinforced by this passage: "And talk meets talk, as echoes from the horn/Of the hunter—echoes are the old men's arts. . . ."

These men are not conversing pragmatically about the immediate work. Presumably one of the echoes is the Civil War as the men tell stories and savor memories. The bold epigrammatic assertion, "echoes are the old men's arts," implies a ripe, civilized nostalgia. "The old endure" because they are capable of this love of their communal past. "Talk meets talk"—the incantatory effect of this is strengthened by the comparison with the hunter's horn. Talk is the auditory embellishment of a serious rite. The last line, "Ample are the chambers of their hearts," is a somewhat pedantic overstatement, a violation of the restrained terseness that is the standard for this poem. A refined humanity is claimed for these men in their imaginative preservation of civilized values, their good faith toward predecessors who sacrificed themselves for an idealism. This clumsily amplifies the theme of durability through good faith.

The simile of the hunter's horn is preparation for the ensuing brief glimpse of a parallel Southern ritual, fox-hunting, a ritual that can embellish cultural nostalgia with bright heraldic colors and graceful motions:

> Here come the hunters, keepers of a rite;
> The horn, the hounds, the lank mares coursing by
> Straddled with archetypes of chivalry;
> And the fox, lovely ritualist, in flight
> Offering his unearthly ghost to quarry;
> And the fields, themselves to harry.

Both the harvesters and the hunters are "keepers of a rite." The precarious chivalric values espoused in this poem can be given a charge of finiteness by the brisk pageantry and sounds of the hunt. Even this Southern recreation is weighted with a traditional symbolic significance. Ransom finds the language to capture this complex mingling of sport and nostalgia, this elusive mystery of social forms and private character.

The description of the "lank mares coursing by/Straddled with archetypes of chivalry" has a complex effect: the colorful, mobile, formally clothed horsemen become a graceful, lyric symbol for Southerners who preserve rituals; the gravely formal phrase, "archetypes of chivalry," attributes a cultural responsibility to these men who keep alive customs that have mysterious overtones of value. The fox is a sacrificial agent in some dimly sensed supernatural order. This is atmospheric preparation for the selfless fidelity which the antique harvesters will invoke for the chivalric Lady. Ransom has found language equal to the extraordinary burden of registering these supernatural overtones.

"Antique Harvesters" is about change and about fidelity to ideals whose permanent validity must be protected if any heroic stand is to be made against cynicism and despair. In the following four stanzas Ransom dramatizes the struggle between the old devotion to something greater than oneself—devotion that involves sacrifice—and the modern commitment to stark practicality and shallow comfort.

Ransom's design calls for language that will express the double sense of a practical, life-sustaining labor and a mysterious ceremony. Harvesting, a pragmatic activity, is clothed with symbolic significance. Color is used to suggest the strange mutability of the crops and the harvesters—and of all things. The bronze of maturity will overtake the green of youth and will be superseded by the gray of old age and death. "Tinge" and "quench" are excellent words for connoting the gradual and gentle natural processes of maturing and dying.

Young Southerners with bronze burdens become a vivid symbolic depiction of the major theme: the need for young men of good faith to carry on the traditions of a mature, humane civilization, even though the civilization seems doomed. Men have their existence in a dreamlike state of changefulness, and time will destroy them; yet they must not succumb to egocentricity but work disinterestedly for "the Lady"—the chivalric patroness, the spirit of the Old South—and thus "prove.../Not less than men." Humanizing customs, these "bronze burdens," are what redeem human life from a stark and cold naturalism, from an utter subservience to change.

Ransom's implication is that the South has had a ripe civilization. There are no hints of illusions about transcending the limitations of life or of restoring the South to its bright youthful state. Young men are called upon to appreciate a stability that has been earned from harsh experience and that is appropriate for a life involved with death, a life that necessitates a constant falling off, a sad diminution. Like Robert Frost in "The Oven Bird," Ransom is walking a precarious line to avoid both a false heroics toward staving off despair and a grim resignation to inevitable decline and destruction. The great achievement of the poem is its tone of quiet courage without bravado, its elusive spirit of patriotism without overstatement.

No extravagant claims are made by the old men. What they offer their sons is the mature pleasure of a social and ancestral continuity throughout the changing periods of their lives. Now the pervasive metaphor of seasons appears again: "And by an autumn tone/As by a grey, as by a green, you will have known/Your famous Lady's image; for so have these. . . ." They will know the South's past—her "green" state—through nostalgic "echoes" if they learn the subtle arts of loyalty, patriotism, and faith. "Grey" in this passage recalls the sacrifice of soldiers in the Civil War. Then comes a glance at the aftermath of the war and the temptations felt by young Southerners to seek comfort and prosperity in the industrial North or to cooperate in accommodating the South to this pernicious 'modernism.'

Ransom strengthened this poem considerably when he added the eighth stanza. The original concluding stanza is uneven. It has the excellent line, "Angry as wasp-music be your cry then," with a simile that produces an original evocation of sound appropriate to anger, and an unusual syntax that sustains the formality of speech in a ritual enactment. But the metaphors for courage and pride—"heart of fire" and "look of snow"—can produce only thin effects because of their triteness. "Dwindled choir" and "Degenerate specters" are deprecating terms that the old men apply to themselves as they urge upon the young men the need for youthful energy in the service of faith. Successors to the faithful elders must bring fresh strength to the pragmatic work—without succumbing to modern pragmatism. "Dwindled choir" too heavily underscores the ritual motif, but the concluding lines of this stanza have a calm and simple dignity of expression that seems right for the ending of the poem. Thematically these lines are climactic, too, suggesting that the young men can preserve the old idealisms and thus be worthy of the heritage that derived from the loving service of their fathers, service that involved the heroic sacrifices of war.

Yet, the eighth stanza is not only a tighter gathering in of the poem's important motifs, but it provides a more powerful climax in the extension of the mysterious logic of faith:

> True, it is said of our Lady, she ageth.
> But see, if you peep shrewdly, she hath not stooped;
> Take no thought of her servitors that have drooped,
> For we are nothing; and if one talk of death—
> Why, the ribs of the earth subsist frail as a breath
> If but God wearieth.

Though the civilization is declining and though its present "servitors" have aged and will soon die, the young men should nevertheless cultivate the redemptive humility and hopeful perseverance. The mysterious, dreamlike quality of existence is dramatically urged again: if the young men face the full logic of an existence that implies a death and are therefore inclined to despair, they should remember that the continuance of the earth itself depends upon God's ability to resist despair. The Lady needs faithful supporters, not immortal ones. What links men to God is not their immortality but their good faith and hopeful endurance under the prospect of death and defeat.

For richness and compression of implied meaning, few modern poems of comparable length can equal "Antique Harvesters." The stylized, sculpture-like fiction of the poem is a ritual enactment. Reverent and patriotic service to a region is allegorized as a noble, humane resistance to change. Ransom undertakes this difficult esthetic purpose mainly by a grave rhetoric designed not only to create and sustain the sacramental atmosphere but to convey precise though complicated ideas.

The first four stanzas present no technical incongruities, except perhaps the deflection from the ritual pattern with the appearance of the fox-hunters. Distracted, the harvesters stop and watch. Although Ransom intuitively knows how to embellish the ritual of harvesting by the grace and color of the hunt, this realistic interruption of the sacramental work is a little amusing and temporarily breaks the atmosphere. Then the heavy-handed Miltonic way of steering our attention back to the laborers—"Resume, harvesters"—shows his design too overtly. The epic tone sounds a little pompous after the distraction.

The lapses into pomposity and verbiage are few. But they *are* lapses; in this poem Ransom does not try to make a self-conscious quaintness serve in the management of tone. Some of the minor flaws could have been expunged by scrupulous revision: the condescending and artificial "Bare the arm, dainty youths," the excrescent "not wholly"—a glaring reminder of the effort to rhyme. The divergence between the weak passages and the great ones needs a narrowing. It is demanded by the sublimity of the ending—an inevitable convergence of idea, emotion, tone, and rhyme: ". . . and if one talk of death—/Why, the ribs of the earth subsist frail as a breath/If but God wearieth." At its best "Antique Harvesters" may be the nearest approximation to the grand style that we have in this century.

CHAPTER 5

Preposterousness and Point:
The Narrative and Whimsical Poems

R EADING THROUGH *Chills and Fever* and *Two Gentle-men in Bonds* will show how much ingenuity Ransom devoted to his narrative and whimsical impulses. Reading in *Selected Poems* the surviving representatives of these formidable impulses will show how infrequently poetry triumphed.

I *Psychological Deflection*

Although the two motives—to tell a story and to perpetrate a drollery—are usually combined, one narrative that benefits greatly from the suppression of whimsy is "Judith of Bethulia." Ransom preserves a serious tone and constructs the poem so that it culminates in a powerful irony. The stringently controlled design is apparent from the very beginning:

> Beautiful as the flying legend of some leopard
> She had not yet chosen her great captain or prince
> Depositary to her flesh, and our defense;
> And a wandering beauty is a blade out of its scabbard.
> You know how dangerous, gentlemen of threescore?
> May you know it yet ten more.

The brilliant analogy for Judith's beauty, "flying legend of some leopard," has an imaginative reach that Ransom does not often achieve. It has the paradoxical quality of great poetry; although it is an indistinct image, it evokes precise feelings about Judith, makes the reader associate an extraordinary woman with a creature of gracefulness and of coordinated, compact strength. It conveys a degree of beauty that cannot be fully expressed by

ordinary language but only by tropes, an idea that will be re-
curred to in the first line of the second stanza with the word
"fabulous." The anomaly of the unmarried status of so prodigious
a woman is gently implied in lines two and three, and then presented in the figure, "a blade out of its scabbard."

"Depositary" is one of Ransom's grave words with rich overtones. "Depositary to her flesh" hints at fidelity and commitment
that fleshly beauty deserves and should exact from a mate. Depositary to "our defense" suggests a conventional way in which
Judith's beauty could benefit her people: she ought to be able
to attract a great warrior or powerful ruler. Ransom's commitment to the formal pattern of question and answer is begun in
this stanza; and the address to the old men, "You know how
dangerous," looks ahead to the major action of the story. The
last line is a superfluous embellishment, a trite and stilted obe-
dience to rhyme.

Stanza two intensifies the beauty of Judith by a clever indirection, by an emphasis upon the erotic unrest that she inspires
in the young men. Again, the language has a sober, elevated
quality: "we were desperate to study/The invincible emanations
of her white body,/And the winds at her ordered raiment were
ominous." No tincture of idle and lighthearted enjoyment of
Judith's sexual charm is permitted to enter the poem. The young
men are gravely afflicted in their desire to see her naked body.
Sobriety of tone is continued in the strange description of the
winds: they are "ominous" because subtle enticements are set
up by the stirring of her veils. Ransom's protection of the tone
from levity is essential to his ultimate emphasis upon the fatal
quality of her beauty, the extraordinary use that can be made of
it and the ironic, solemn consequences for her.

Probably the poem's least effective lines constitute the third
stanza. Narration becomes abrupt, expression undistinguished.
Even the metaphor of beauty as a deadly weapon seems flat and
colorless in this context, following as it does so inevitably the
description of Holofernes and his great army bearing down upon
the city: "Where were the arms could countervail this horde?/
Her beauty was the sword."

One surprising effect of this poem is our discovery that
Ransom will not exploit the most dramatic act, the beheading of
Holofernes. Incident does not predominate; narrative serves a

subtler purpose. As we gradually perceive that Ransom's motive is to extract an intense irony from the story, we assent to the persistent recurrence to Judith's extraordinary "sword" and the casual suppression of the most melodramatic event:

> She sat with the elders, and proved on their blear visage
> How bright was the weapon unrusted in her keeping,
> While he lay surfeiting on their harvest heaping,
> Wasting the husbandry of their rarest vintage—
> And dreaming of the broad-breasted dames for concubine?
> These floated on his wine.

> He was lapped with bay-leaves, and grass and fumiter weed,
> And from under the wine-film encountered his mortal vision,
> For even within his tent she accomplished his derision;
> She loosed one veil and another, standing unafraid;
> And he perished. Nor brushed her with even so much as a daisy?
> She found his destruction easy.

Holofernes' awful susceptibility is richly portrayed. In the victory celebration, the conqueror's appetites mingle gloriously; while he enjoys the food and wine, he anticipates the lusty pleasures to follow. Ransom admirably conveys the sensual euphoria: "broad-breasted dames... floated on his wine." This is one of the best stanza endings. The rhythm of the terse declaration is very pleasing in conjunction with the bold metaphoric ingenuity to capture the mood of a man savoring his satieties and permitting them to blur into one another so luxuriously.

There has been a nice preparation for the line, "And from under the wine-film encountered his mortal vision." The word "mortal" gently works against the self-indulgent mood of Holofernes. He sees the disrobing of Judith as a lovely culmination of his joy; and, surrendering to the "vision" and to the appearance of feminine passivity, he is unprepared for her savage action. Thus her beauty *has* been a subtle—because implausible—weapon.

The ensuing events are related with swiftness and economy: "We smote them hiding in our vineyards, barns, annexes,/And now their white bones clutter the holes of foxes...." The question-and-answer pattern rises to a quiet intensity:

And the chieftain's head, with grinning sockets, and varnished—
Is it hung on the sky with a hideous epitaphy?
No, the woman keeps the trophy.

Violent change of fortune is suggested by the contrast between
Holofernes in glorious anticipation of pleasure and the remaining
"varnished" head, but the emphasis of the question and answer
falls upon the characterization of Judith. Her calm detachment
upon her incredible act of violence is conveyed by "trophy."
With this word, the poem's thematic point begins to emerge:
accompanying the extraordinary beauty of Judith is an incongruous brutality.

Now Ransom is ready to return to the idea so plausibly set
forth in the first stanza, that so beautiful a woman ought to
have a husband. But we cannot now entertain the suggestion so
blithely, for our accrual of information about Judith gives it an
ironic cast. The poem ends with a splendid underscoring of the
paradox which has been hinted at from the beginning but which
is delicately sharpened here:

May God send unto our virtuous lady her prince.
It is stated she went reluctant to that orgy,
Yet a madness fevers our young men, and not the clergy
Nor the elders have turned them unto modesty since.
Inflamed by the thought of her naked beauty with desire?
Yes, and chilled with fear and despair.

These young men cannot help imagining the rare pleasure of
Holofernes when he saw Judith naked; so their obsession with
her beauty is intensified. But they cannot now have an unalloyed
phantasy of her; the erotic delirium is harshly qualified by their
sense of her deadly brutality, her fierceness that is so inimical
to feminine loveliness. Judith the enticing beauty must be permanently associated in their imaginations with Judith the cool
murderer who keeps the varnished head of her victim.

Assuming a sophisticated reader who knows the story of
Judith and Holofernes, Ransom has tried not merely to retell
the story in a fresh way but to deflect the reader's attention from
exciting incident and toward psychological consequence. Judith
served her community bravely and uncompromisingly; but, in
her wholehearted commitment to a perverted use of beauty, she

subtlety, a quietly aggressive, self-conscious assertion of poetic autonomy. What could the motive be but an implausible 'purity,' an effort to ride a poem solely on nebulous comedy? The worst specimens, I fear, have the greatest autonomy. When nothing but whimsy can be found the poem is usually embarrassing. Whimsy as atmosphere, however, *can* lead to a pleasing effect: the reader experiences a gradual discovery that his initial surrender to the fancy has made him vulnerable to a serious theme.

Two poems about Christianity illustrate Ransom's erratic control over the technique of high-spirited comedy. Both seem to beckon as harmless excursions into absurdity, but one carries the reader toward a surprising relevance. "Our Two Worthies" is the result of persistence in an abortive idea; "Armageddon" begins with a bold dramatization that invites some extravagant refinements. "Our Two Worthies" is not organized for an incisive narrative purpose; it develops haphazardly. The opening is unfortunate not only because it is stodgy but because it indicates how verbally unambitious the poem will be. Ransom compromises immediately with a tone of triviality and with a meager wittiness confined to rhyme:

> All the here and all the there
> Ring with the praises of the pair:
> Jesus the Paraclete
> And Saint Paul the Exegete.

Paul's mission as the scholarly interpreter and proselytizer of Christianity is now described by an absurd conceit, a mixture of mastication and digestion with cookery and drug manufacture. Nothing mitigates the strained humor; rhyme continues obvious and often feminine:

> Jesus proclaimed the truth.
> Paul's missionary tooth
> Shredded it fine, and made a paste,
> No particle going to waste,
> Kneaded it and caked it
> And buttered it and baked it
> (And indeed all but digested
> While Jesus went to death and rested)

> Into a marketable compound
> Ready to lay on any wound,
> Meet to prescribe to our distress
> And feed unto our emptiness.

Labored extensions and weak repetitions dilute what, with some restraint, might have been an amusing motif. Further obtrusiveness results from the forced archaic diction, "Meet to" and "feed unto."

Although the heavy effects persist, the next four-line stanza introduces the Christian emphasis upon perfection and incorporeality as the panacea for all human ills, and prepares for these four lines, one of the two admirable passages of the poem:

> When the great captains die,
> There is some faithful standing by
> To whom the chieftain hands his sword.
> Proud Paul received—a Word.

Our good faith in the poem receives a momentary justification as Ransom summons this apt analogy to the aid of meager poetic resources. With impressive economy and telling rhyme he implies Paul's militancy in the paradoxical service of Christian immateriality. This is the first amusing stroke that rises above the quality of doggerel. The only other deviation into poetry occurs with this flash of wit in the next stanza:

> He blessed the mighty Paraclete
> For needing him, to miss defeat,
> He couldn't have done anything
> But for his Captain spiriting.

"But for his Captain spiriting" is the most brilliant line of the poem. It carries out the motif of a military commander handing on his authority to a trusted lieutenant, and, with the word "spiriting," the line deftly establishes both the picture of a captain running away from battle and the idea of Christ's departure from a fleshly state. Furthermore, the standard meaning of "spiriting" is relevant here: providing inspiration.

The rest of the poem is an anticlimactic return to the strain and poverty of the early lines, to the dubious reliance upon denotation embellished by obvious rhyme. A weak hyperbole has Satan fearing the powers of Paul's rhetorical "spell"; then the conclusion is made with a transparent parody of a catechism. A durable humor demands tighter control. Ransom has an excellent ironical idea—that Paul owes his fame to the *incompleteness* of Christ's work—but he does not carry his reader gently and skillfully toward a culminating subtlety of awareness. The art is only sporadic and short-lived.

In "Armageddon," however, invention is not fortuitous. A thematic purpose controls the selection of amusing incidents and the delicate turns of characterization. It is evident from the opening lines that economy and point are working. Ransom casts Christ and Antichrist as exemplars of asceticism and worldliness, respectively; and their characteristic tones are caught at once:

> Antichrist, playing his lissome flute and merry
> As was his wont, debouched upon the plain;
> Then came a swirl of dust, and Christ drew rein,
> Brooding upon his frugal breviary.

The opposed claims of joy and conscientiousness are quietly announced in a pattern of economy and connotation. Antichrist arrives on the scene engulfed in spontaneous music, whereas Christ is engaging in directed and prescribed study. "Lissome flute" and "frugal breviary" swiftly establish the polarities. They are sounded again in the following stanza with "the roundel, rose, and hall" and "the tonsured beadsman's monkery."

Now begins the gradual extraction of irony from these two uncompromising attitudes toward existence. Antichrist has wrought some delicacies from his worldly interests; he has nurtured some subtle arts and gentle social conventions. His courtesy impels him to renounce any advantage in the contest with his adversary, to prostrate himself before Christ and give up the superior horse:

> But Antichrist got down from the Barbary beast
> And doffed his plume in courteous prostration;
> Christ left his jennet's back in deprecation
> And raised him, his own hand about the waist.
>
> Then next they fingered chivalry's quaint page,
> Of precedence discoursing by the letter.
> The oratory of Antichrist was better,
> He invested Christ with the elder lineage.

In this poem Ransom's preservation of a medieval atmosphere is not a self-indulgence but an appropriate and rich embellishment of theme. The deliberate archaisms, inversions, and chivalric rituals become quite relevant when we see an analogy to "The Franklin's Tale" of Chaucer in the unexpected conflict that erupts over which combatant shall be allowed to exhibit the more courtesy. Antichrist prevails because of his superiority in the secular art of oratory. Here Ransom deftly introduces the amusing dilemma which he will attenuate. Fancy does not become anarchic and nonsensical; the fictional narrative is nicely subordinate to the production of humor through subtle extensions of the dilemma. We begin with something traditionally plausible, the staging of a much-prophesied battle. Furthermore, the preëminent traits which are ascribed to Christ—kindness and gentleness—make no exorbitant demand upon the reader's credulity. Ransom's invention will be applied to dramatizing the spectacle and the traits.

The motif of a battle yields a humorous incongruity in one stanza—Christ's appearance as a physical warrior:

> He set Christ on his own Mahomet's back
> Where Christ sat fortressed up like Diomede;
> The cynical hairy jennet was his steed,
> Obtuse, and most indifferent to attack.

If there is to be a *battle* of Armageddon, then somebody representing the forces of good must fight it; but perhaps the struggle must be kept abstract and visionary if it is to be taken seriously. Ransom creates humor simply by treating concretely the preparations for battle, by describing the Prince of Peace on a war horse.

After Christ finds himself the beneficiary of Antichrist's magnanimity, He would be a churl indeed to seize the advantage and immediately attack his opponent. He has been given a plausible motive to conciliate the "honorable dispute." This ceremony enables Ransom to exploit some temperamental biases in the two adversaries. Christ, too, would like to be magnanimous. His idealism and gentleness extend even to a desire to abate his moral rigor, his social inflexibility; but he is unschooled in the amenities. Antichrist, habitually at ease and graceful in manners, gives Christ "a spray of rosemary/To serve his brother for a buttonhole," whereupon Christ produces "a dry palm that grew on Calvary." Christ's temperamental gravity and his incapacity to perform a simple courtesy free of weighty symbolism are admirably depicted.

Ransom glances at other secular pleasures and implies the discomfiture of Christ caused by showy clothing: "his egregious beauty richly dight"; by intoxicating drink: "Christ, introducing water in the liquor,/Made wine of more ethereal bouquet"; by singing: "Christ beat the time, and hummed a stave or two,/But did not say the words, which were profane"; by hair-dressing:

> Perruquiers were privily presented,
> Till, knowing his need extreme and his heart pure,
> Christ let them dress him his thick chevelure,
> And soon his beard was glozed and sweetly scented.

The witty point is a puritan's squeamishness and scrupulosity over possible corruptions. Christ was aware of his disheveled hair ("Knowing his need extreme"), and he saw no danger of vanity in having it dressed (knowing "his heart pure").

Every stanza has contributed to Ransom's sly notion that politeness—chivalric courtesy—is the point of greatest harmony between Christ and Antichrist. A rich and massive versification marks this dramatic moment:

> And so the Wolf said Brother to the Lamb,
> The True Heir keeping with the poor Impostor,
> The rubric and the holy paternoster
> Were jangled strangely with the dithyramb.

Versatile language is required to sustain the seemingly incompatible ends of the poem. In this stanza is the elusive combination of whimsy and elevation that Ransom must have sought in his persistent efforts to transmute his fanciful materials into poetry.

The activities that Ransom extracts humor from keep relating themselves to the ambiguities in good and evil as they are precariously known by human beings—the virtue that is often gauche, narrow, and rigid; the vice that often strangely fosters grace, art, and flexibility. Secular gracefulness and pious magnanimity are the bases of community and harmony between the two antagonists. Ransom pushes his controlling ironical idea as far as he can when he has a conservative patriarch, intent upon recalling his leader to the proper strictness, confound the identities and deliver his complaint to Antichrist. This extraordinary confusion dramatizes for Christ the sinister implications of his venture into flexibility and charity, and makes him abruptly renounce all the outward signs of his polite cooperation with the enemy. He gives up the splendid clothing for his smock, "smears himself" with ashes, applies the scourge, and takes back his jennet.

Now Ransom can move swiftly to the climactic inconsistency. Recalled to "right opinions," Christ becomes outwardly warlike, chanting of "death and glory and no complaisance"—with a devotion to principle that is quite unchristian in its harsh completeness. The "glory" here is that of military triumph. The characteristic roles are reversed; while Christ and his followers thunder like bloodthirsty secularists, Antichrist and his armies make "songs of innocence and no bloodshed." A brilliant piece of casuistry has been saved for the ending. With a witty emphasis upon Antichrist's incapacity to sustain a principle, even against his uncompromising enemy, Ransom leaves us to make the inference that a struggle between Christ and Antichrist can only be academic because of Antichrist's radical lack of character: he cannot manage even a devotion to infamous ideals. At the moment when he should take the field against his adversary, he is preoccupied by a fear that he would get hungry during a protracted struggle; and he is squeamish at the sight of blood. It is a splendid paradoxical conclusion: Christ is so worked up on behalf of moral consistency that he is ready to violate his cardinal virtues of charity and peace; Antichrist is so uncommitted to any principle that he is bored by the spectacular cosmic engagement.

"Armageddon" is one of the three poems that vindicate Ransom's momentous faith in whimsicality as a technique for protecting the author's 'anonymity' and for insuring against a naïve, sober presentation of an idea. Perhaps its idea does not invite a wholly serious response; however, Ransom's ingenuity is given direction and kept under control by an intellectual motive, an insistence upon the alloyed quality of good and evil that would preclude any ultimate confrontation and struggle. The strategy for generating comedy is a playful casuistry that refuses to consider good and evil in any purer form than that which they have assumed in human experience.

In "Philomela" Ransom works through hyperbole and caricature to imply a gross deficiency in the American sensibility, and in "Captain Carpenter" he entices the reader with a ludicrous surrealism that gradually leads to an appalling view of reality. That "Philomela" will not be a vague surrender to comic impulse is evident from the thematic hint in the opening stanza; control is exerted by Ransom's motive of defining a negative American trait:

> Procne, Philomela, and Itylus,
> Your names are liquid, your improbable tale
> Is recited in the classic numbers of the nightingale.
> Ah, but our numbers are not felicitous,
> It goes not liquidly for us.

Too dark and melancholy a tale cannot be intuitively felt by Americans; in contrast, the different peoples of Europe have assimilated it. As a figurative way of showing the receptiveness of Europeans to the somber tale, Ransom now gives a quick historical survey of the fate of the nightingale after she was doomed to flee from Tereus. Leaving Greece, she found some hospitality among the Romans. She was accommodated even by the heavy, phlegmatic German sensibility ("the swilled and gravid"). Ransom can make a fine rhyming distinction with his treatment of the French: the nightingale may have been "gallicized," but "Never was she baptized." Perhaps this line implies that a pagan spirit is indispensable, a spirit that enables even the English to respond to the mysterious "untranslatable refrain."

Americans, however, are too committed to the realities of sunlight. Distracted by their simplified political doctrines, they suppress lyric intuitions of melancholy. Ransom is implicitly charging that Whitman's version of America has prevailed, not Poe's or Hawthorne's or Melville's:

> Not to these shores she came! this other Thrace,
> Environ barbarous to the royal Attic;
> How could her delicate dirge run democratic,
> Delivered in a cloudless boundless public place
> To an inordinate race?

Exactly in the middle of the poem Ransom shifts to a bold personal exemplum that enables him to clinch the point and to make a dramatic conclusion. He casts himself as a culturally undernourished American trying to make Oxford yield him her subtleties:

> I pernoctated with the Oxford students once,
> And in the quadrangles, in the cloisters, on the Cher,
> Precociously knocked at antique doors ajar,
> Fatuously touched the hems of the hierophants,
> Sick of my dissonance.

This unusual diction is not an aimless indulgence in archaism and fancy; "pernoctated" is an excellent comic word for night-time contemplation, and its pedantic overtone is quite appropriate. "Precociously knocked at antique doors ajar" hints at the rawness and cultural ineptitude of the young American student too stolidly engaging ancient European secrets. "Sick of my dissonance" is a gentle thematic underscoring: the American longs to transcend his provincialism and to register some esoteric nuances. This self-dissatisfaction is echoed in the next stanza with the line, "There was no more villainous day to unfulfil." Daylight is associated with American limitations, American harshnesses.

Now Ransom is ready for his caricature of himself as a large-eared American rustic, self-consciously straining to hear cultural overtones:

> Up from the darkest wood where Philomela sat,
> Her fairy numbers issued. What then ailed me?
> My ears are called capacious but they failed me,
> Her classics registered a little flat!
> I rose, and venomously spat.

With an impatient gesture of futility, the awkward pilgrim abandons his quest, suddenly resigns himself to American inadequacy. America is too coarse, too committed to a shallow modernity; it is not "young," not receptive to the elusive music and subtle ingenuousness of European poetic myths:

> Philomela, Philomela, lover of song,
> I am in despair if we may make us worthy,
> A bantering breed, sophistical and swarthy;
> Unto more beautiful, persistently more young,
> Thy fabulous provinces belong.

"Philomela" has the retroactive impact that Ransom values. After we have absorbed the immediate data—the bird and its travels, the rustic and his efforts to hear an exotic song—we find that they do not seem obtrusive and farfetched; rather, they function as an efficient indirection, as a little parable for the void in the American sensibility. Ransom has the principled satisfaction of conveying his idea to the reader by a playful, apparently innocent, little story about the nightingale's wanderings and about the modern American's effort to register a foreign lyricism. The ultimate success of this kind of poem lies in whether it gives the reader an original, memorable sense of an abstraction, whether it transcends the explicit details of the fable.

IV *Consummation of the Technique*

Anyone familiar with, and dismayed by, the great number of ill-formed and irresolute caprices among Ransom's poems will know how to value "Captain Carpenter." This poem is the consummation of an indefatigable pursuit of whimsy as a poetic technique. The invention turns out to be, in retrospect, hauntingly purposeful; it is directed by an allegorical motive of the kind that informs some of Stephen Crane's little epitomes of the human obsession with ideals that the world frustrates. Ransom's splendid comic sense insures against a sentimental portrait of the captain, but the peculiar triumph of this work—and its great difference from Crane's allegories—is that some sympathy accrues for the absurd hero who can persevere in the life of passionate commitment and action even though he experiences defeat after defeat.

"Captain Carpenter" immediately announces itself as an incredible tale. The ballad-like straightforwardness of presentation, the mannered syntax, and the extravagantly archaic diction contribute to the reader's sense of an innocuous, diverting story. From the first line, Ransom's strategy is to provide an atmosphere of pure feigning. All of the outward signs are that the reader should surrender to the pleasure of pure incident.

> Captain Carpenter rose up in his prime
> Put on his pistols and went riding out
> But had got wellnigh nowhere at that time
> Till he fell in with ladies in a rout.

The narrative conventionality of "rose up in his prime" and "had got wellnigh nowhere at that time" is so extreme that no one would be tempted to reflect carefully upon the words, to look for significance beyond the account of events. An ancient storytelling locution begins the next stanza:

> It was a pretty lady and all her train
> That played with him so sweetly but before
> An hour she'd taken a sword with all her main
> And twined him of his nose for evermore.

Every line contributes to the exaggerated conventionality of narration: "It was a pretty lady," "That played with him so sweetly," "with all her main," "twined him of his nose for ever- more." This fictional style, so ingenuous and innocent, gently encourages the reader to accept the outrageous events in the captain's life with equanimity, even with an irresistible perverse amusement. But, if the poem is not to be limited to a detached and quaint riot of fancy, Ransom must craftily transmit serious implications through the patently comic presentation. One source of esthetic suspense here lies in whether the stylized locutions and the archaisms will turn out merely to bespeak a poet's ec- centricities or whether they will quietly create atmosphere and distract the reader from expecting a sober theme.

Ransom is practicing a delicate art in this poem. Some of his most pleasurable strokes are little extensions of absurdity and lit- tle ironic relevances. The captain's vague idealism is nicely sug- gested by the account of his attack upon a man who is wholly unfamiliar to him, "a stranger rogue"; but the obscurantist motive is made more absurd by the phrase, "that looked unchristian." A fine grotesque pun is exploited in the taunt of the wife of Satan: "'I'm/The she-wolf bids you shall bear no more arms.'" Some- times the sheer phrasing creates the absurd effect: "Their strokes and counters whistled in the wind." "Whistled" is the perfect word to preserve the comic tone, and no verb could enhance the ridiculous humiliation of the captain as well as the word "bit" in this passage: "But where she should have made off like a hind/ The bitch bit off his arms at the elbows." Ransom pushes beyond ludicrous incident into grotesque characterization when he has the captain—after suffering two broken legs and losing his nose, ears, and eyes—speak belligerently, asking, "If any enemy yet there was to fight." This lovely bombast continues, and culminates in the word "perils":

> "To any adversary it is fame
> If he risk to be wounded by my tongue
> Or burnt in two beneath my red heart's flame
> Such are the perils he is cast among."

These are the exquisite effects that Ransom coveted but could not often achieve. How implausible as a source of comedy is the grim accuracy of "an anatomy with little to lose." How astonishing is the comic power of the innocuous phrase "if they can" in this line: "Let jangling kites eat of him if they can."

Inevitably, though, a strange uneasiness must attend the reader's enjoyment of this comic starkness; for, despite the preservation of the narrative conventionality and the stylized invocations—"But God's deep curses follow after those . . ." and "The curse of hell upon the sleek upstart . . ."—there develops a persistent feeling that, because of the thoroughness of his defeat and failure, the captain deserves some sympathy, and that it is a form of debauchery to laugh at him purely. Protection against sentimentality is complete, yet a legitimate feeling of pathos emerges. The concluding line—"And made the kites to whet their beaks clack clack"—carries this terrible ambiguity, emphasizing the ultimate ignoble fact of human existence: that courage and idealism issue in the same outrageous naturalistic destiny as cowardice and cynicism. The most formidable irony of the captain's career is that he is killed not by a hearty warrior but by an overrefined worldling, an Osric, "the neatest knave that ever was seen/Stepping in perfume from his lady's bower."

"Captain Carpenter" is like "Judith of Bethulia" in its sharp narrative pattern and in its deft exploitation of story as a sly means of indirection. From the steady, gradual accretion of information comes an intensity, as well as a weird, strangely

heightened commingling of comic absurdity and sad adversity.
The patent exaggerations, bolstered by an ancient narrative style
and by persistent archaic expression, lull the reader into the
serene expectation of a diverting comedy. And, though the absurdity can be enjoyed for its own sake at first, the reader must
see in retrospect that Ransom has held it in firm subordination
to an awful irony of existence. To give this old irony an original
embodiment and to deliver it with powerful impact are Ransom's consistent aims.

The poem is at once about the inevitable defeat of human
idealism and about the incredible triumph of good faith. Irony
here is not of the sickly kind that pervades many of Ransom's
treatments of emotional paralysis. Captain Carpenter is the
splendid and ridiculous victim of outrages suffered because of
his committed participation in life. He is an absurd figure precisely because he does not despair when the number and extent
of his defeats should overwhelm him. Ransom's structure is designed to produce an extraordinary amusement of logic: the
captain preserves his spiritual essence—his faith and hope—in
spite of the gradual loss of important parts of his anatomy; and,
before each new encounter with an adversary, he behaves not
like a man whose crushing defeats and physical losses have made
him tentative and wary but like a man whose whole experience
has been with victory and fulfillment. His nobility consists of his
immunity to despair, his utter imperviousness to the dreadful
humiliations that he keeps asking for.

No poem of Ransom's creates such an inspired illusion of
phantasmagoria as this one. From the steadily increasing dis-
memberment emerges a powerful surrealistic violence which
propels the reader into a hallucinated sense of the polar human
obsessions, faith and futility. In a pattern of gentle, innocent,
comic narration, both realities are set forth with a savage, uncompromising completeness so that we may not reflect upon
them separately, so that we are compelled to envision the magnificent and horrifying ambiguity of existence.

CHAPTER 6

Ransom the Revisionist

A PROPER appreciation of Ransom's poetry calls for a modest cultivation of literary asceticism. The reader must accustom himself to the idea that he will encounter no portrayal of strong personalities, no mighty emotional drama, and (except very faintly and indirectly) little sense of a poet's dreadful self-discovery. He must tune himself to register elusive subtleties of perception and elegances of rhyme, wit, and rhetoric. He must be somewhat willing to forgive Ransom for the acute esthetic self-consciousness that made him habitually subordinate passion to tonal control. He must be indulgent of Ransom's addictions to pale or paralyzing irony and to refined whimsicality. In brief, he should accept the limitations inherent in a civilized poetry and try to savor the fragile excellences.

The most dramatic growth of Ransom's sensibility and artistic conscience occurred between 1919 and 1924, the publication dates of *Poems About God* and *Chills and Fever*. *Poems About God* reflect a serene amateurism of directness, a naïve faith in the exploitation of the poet's personality. With *Chills and Fever* come the revulsion against sentimentality and the parallel obsession with the doctrine of esthetic distance. The primitive ideal of raw and undifferentiated emotion is replaced with the civilized ideal of the precise emotion in the appropriate degree and in a decorous presentation.

This militant program for curbing emotional overstatement and naïve perspective leads to fresh experimentation in the control of tone, and some of the results are impressive. Ransom has poems that rank with the very best civilized poetry in English. Inevitably, though, throughout the collections *Chills and Fever* and *Two Gentlemen in Bonds* (1927) appear many items that are no more than unintentional parodies of civilized poetry. They interest us today as strange specimens of an anti-Victorian bias, little exercises in tepidness and contrivance, the ingenious sub-version of legitimate human feeling by a preoccupation with modernist technique.

Consistent with the scrupulous standards that Ransom adopted for his poetics was the tacit desire to be represented by a selection of his poems. He brought out in 1945 the first *Selected Poems,* then in 1955 a slightly revised edition in paperback (with some essays in criticism), and in 1963 the most extensively revised and expanded version. Because he has been at the exacting, self-defensive work of selection and revision three times, he should expect us to judge his volume meticulously, with less magnanimity than we might extend to Frost, say, who chose to be represented by a fat book and, shunning the delicate arts of exclusion and reconsideration, left in his meager poems and his self-indulgent exercises in drollery and triviality.

I *Exclusion and Refinement in 1945*

After *Two Gentlemen in Bonds* only a little of Ransom's creative energy went into the writing of new poems. His love of modest perfections kept him at work revising his selected poems, and any evaluation of him must take into account these local improvements, the little tightenings and recastings that result in positive strengthening of the poems or at least in mitigating the most obtrusive and lamentable eccentricities. Fastidious principles govern the early revisions.

Often Ransom sharply hunts down the word that calls attention to itself for a negative reason. The reader's imaginative participation in a poem may be halted both by overstatement, or floridity, and by the counterheresy, flat and meager denotation. Often the revisions enhance the atmosphere of a poem; words that say everything bluntly are replaced by words that carry overtones. "Spectral Lovers" has undergone this kind of improvement. Two lines in the original,

> As out of the rich ground strangely come to birth,
> Else two immaculate angels fallen on earth,

are changed for the 1945 edition of *Selected Poems* to

> Out of that black ground suddenly come to birth,
> Else angels lost in each other and fallen on earth.

"Rich ground" does not suggest a hellish origin as "black ground" does. "Rich" has no relevant connotations; "black" contributes to the atmosphere while suggesting the antithesis to a heavenly origin. "Strangely" is flat, repetitious of what is implicit. "Suddenly" contributes to the supernatural atmosphere that is used for an ironic purpose in this poem, to suggest that these lovers deny their bodies so effectually and completely that they could not possibly have the same origin as natural human beings. "Immaculate" is superfluous because its meaning is implicit in "angels." Elimination of this word permits the inclusion of "lost in each other," a much more controlled description that does not naïvely surrender to the figure of speech and, therefore, does not distract the reader from attending to these people as *earthly* lovers paralyzed by ideals. Emphasis falls upon their raptness, their exclusive absorption in one another. The figure is designed to dramatize their strange appearance, the extraordinary restrained behavior. "Her thrilling fingers touched him quick with care" becomes "Scarcely her fingers touched him, quick with care." Again an exhaustive denotation—"thrilling"—is eliminated, and the new word—"Scarcely"—permits an association with the metaphor of angels, strengthening the emphasis upon the lovers' unnatural separateness.

The admirable sonnet, "Good Ships," is strengthened by the suppression of the abstract, denotative word "eternity." "Fleet ships encountering on the high seas/Who speak, and unto eternity diverge—" is altered to "unto the vast diverge"; and, although "the vast" is not more concrete than "eternity," it subtly contributes to the conceit of sailing while suggesting the uncertainty of the future without the excessive gravity of "eternity."

Ransom's scrupulous attention to false diction leads to a slight change in "Dead Boy" that has important consequences. Originally the concluding lines of the first stanza read "And neither the county kin love the transaction/Nor some of the world of outer dark, like me." "*Love* the transaction" too obviously underscores the irony. Furthermore, "like" is better suited to the objectivity of the metaphor of trading.

It is a very good sign of alertness when a poet detects and removes quiet bombast. Noisy bombast is easy to find: the slight poem "Her Eyes" is changed for the better with the removal of an excessively negative metaphor, "Painted pigsties," and the substitution of a more decorous complaint, "They are lies." Similarly, the single revised line of "Miriam Tazewell" is a resistance to flamboyant language. Here is the original concluding stanza:

> To Miriam Tazewell the whole world was villain,
> To prosper when the fragile babes were fallen;
> The principle of the beast was low and masculine!
> For weeks she went untidy, she went sullen.

The revised version suppresses the melodramatic third line, which is really a heavy-handed ironic interjection by the author to convey Miriam's feminist prejudice—a lapse in the narration—and replaces it with this quieter, gently cohering line: "And not to unstop her own storm and be maudlin." Our attention is now directed to Miriam, as the metaphor of her interior storm is related to the destructive weather that has provoked her embittered response.

Ransom worked heroically against the incredible bombast of the original "Vaunting Oak" to prepare it for the first *Selected Poems*. He threw out two stanzas that were easily the most ludicrous:

> But he casts the feeble generations of leaf,
> And naked to the spleen of the cold skies eruptive
> That howl on his defiant head in chief,
>
> Bears out their frenzy to its period,
> And hears in the spring, a little more rheumy and deaf,
> After the tragedy the lyric palinode. . . .

In this poem bloated language is supposed to serve the ends of an elaborate whimsicality. I consider the whole work a misconception that calls for suppression, not mere revision; but Ransom did unerringly fix upon and remove the silliest lines, this absurd refinement upon the personification of the tree. Pedantic pomposity is a dubious source of esthetic distance, especially when the farcical tone is abruptly dropped and the concluding three stanzas made to evoke a grave sadness. This is Ransom's studiously fanciful method of avoiding sentimentality, and it is the least satisfactory way. But, even in this poem, his revisions are telling; lessenings of the rhetorical absurdity are worth something. Rhythm as well as tone is improved when this passage,

> But he may break
> If Heaven in a rage try him too windily,

is changed to

> But how will he not break,
> If Heaven assault him with full wind and sleet. . . .

The two best phrases of the poem—"phantasy of good" and "instructed of much mortality"—result from revision. The original line, "And she exulted—being given to crying," becomes "And exulted, wrapped in a phantasy of good." The original line, "Who had sorely been instructed of much decease," becomes "Who had been instructed of much mortality."

Some improvements result from the excision of gross and heavy 'poetic' effects. From this line of the original "Blue Girls," "Tie the white fillets then about your lustrous hair," the decorative "lustrous" disappears. In "Dead Boy" the obtrusive diction, "Aggrieving the sapless limbs," yields to the usual form, "Grieving the sapless limbs," without any damage to the meter or to the sober tone.

Originally "Spectral Lovers" had much of this self-conscious preciosity. "Of many delicate postures she cast a snare" becomes in 1945 "Yet of evasions even she made a snare." Strained, artificial expression is gone; the idea is clearer; a greater complexity is captured—the girl's awareness that she can coyly exploit an apparent distraction, "the shredding of an April blossom," to encourage the man's sexual attention. With the change of the line "But for all the red heart beating in the pale bosom" to "The heart was bold that clanged within her bosom," the forced 'poetic' use of color, that is merely decorative, is deleted and replaced by a memorable figure that uses sound to evoke strength of emotion. "Clanged" is excellent for suggesting the bold risk the girl is willing to take, to "surrender all." In the last stanza of the original version the spectral lovers are described as "Trailing a glory of moon-gold and amethyst." This vague and contrived embellishment is transmuted into a lovely, economical use of color that enhances both atmosphere and theme: "White in the season's moon-gold and amethyst." This description quietly creates an ironic contrast between the rich colors of the environment that the "White" lovers—bloodless in their restraint—are unable to live up to.

One of the most difficult of self-imposed restraints for Ransom must be the curbing of old-fashioned language. Archaisms appear often in his early collections, and frequently they are artificial and gratuitous, not functional. In "Spectral Lovers" for 1945 he judiciously changed the phrase "frozen asunder" to "frozen apart." However, in "Necrological" he improves a phrase by importing an archaism. These lines appear near the end of the original: "The youth possessed him then of a crooked blade/ Deep in the belly of a lugubrious knight"; and in 1945 "knight" is changed to "wight," a more conspicuous 'medieval' word that carries with it a greater forlornness, the sad anonymity created by death.

The motive of increased precision inspires a change of one word in a splendid Oriental trope of "Necrological": "In defeat the heroes' bosoms were whitely bare,/The field was white like meads of asphodel." With the substitution of "bodies" for "bosoms," the amount of whiteness is immediately doubled or tripled. This suits better with the trope, "meads of asphodel." Tonal improvement results, too, from the elimination of the preciosity and of the overt pathos in the naming of masculine chests.

Precise syntactical tightening and the addition of the word "cold" provide an enhanced atmosphere of death for the ending of "Puncture." The original reads: "Smoke and a dry word crackled from his mouth/And the wind ferried them South"; the 1945 version: "Smoke and a dry word crackled from his mouth/ Which a cold wind ferried south."

Probably the subtlest changes which Ransom made for 1945 facilitate our swift insight into the psychology of his characters. This passage in "Puncture"—"I would not weep, and like a desperado/Kicked on the carcasses of our enemies . . ."—becomes a richer datum of the narrator's psychology with the simple change to "I, not to weep then, like a desperado/Kicked on the carcasses of our enemies. . . ." Now we infer that the narrator commits this act of indignity as an alternative to sitting there and succumbing to the grief that he feels over Grimes's mortal wound. He must do something, though no action is appropriate under the circumstances. He has the right emotion, but he expresses it in a gross and barbarous way and provokes a rebuke from Grimes. The implication is that the civilized Grimes is thus impelled to utter his last word and it turns out to be a defense of the 'courtesies.'

A single change in "Emily Hardcastle, Spinster" brings in a fine psychological precision. The narrator, one of the local suitors of Emily, reveals the casual cynicism of himself and the other young men (the "local beauties") toward her idealistic standards for marriage. They expected her to tire of spinsterhood, to compromise her standards, and to settle for one of them. The early version reads: "We were only local beauties, and we beautifully trusted/If the proud one had to tarry we would take her by default." The 1945 version substitutes "have" for "take," implying a passivity in the suitors. They are not as vigorous and aggressive as the "Grizzled Baron."

In the original "Janet Waking" the girl is described as "Running on little pink feet upon the grass." The revision for 1945, "Running across the world upon the grass," not only eliminates trite and overt sentimentality but provides a startling metaphysical image that induces empathy with Janet's psychological perspective.

The most ambitious and probably the most brilliant change for the 1945 *Selected Poems* was the addition of a whole new stanza at the end of "Antique Harvesters":

> True, it is said of our Lady, she ageth.
> But see, if you peep shrewdly, she hath not stooped;
> Take no thought of her servitors that have drooped,
> For we are nothing; and if one talk of death—
> Why, the ribs of the earth subsist frail as a breath
> If but God wearieth.

This admirable cosmic extension of the poem's theme creates a much more powerful ending than the preceding stanza did. Young Southerners are urged to resist despair and to be loyal and faithful to the South even during her decline. The implication is that, though the creation of humanity may not always thrive, God does not abandon his enterprise. This bold and grave analogy gives the poem a startling climax.

II Reconsiderations in 1955

The *Selected Poems* of 1945 was the occasion for Ransom's best revisions. Although the ones made for *Poems and Essays* of 1955 reflect the same esthetic scruples, they are not as consistently excellent. "Emily Hardcastle, Spinster" is strengthened by some changes in the last stanza. In 1945:

> But right across her threshold has the Grizzled Baron come.
> Let them wrap her as a princess, who would patter down a stairway
> Where the foreigner may take her for his gloomy halidom.

In 1955:

> But right across her threshold has her Grizzled Baron come;
> Let them wrap her as a princess, who'd go softly down a stairway
> And seal her to the stranger for his castle in the gloom.

These are subtle enrichments of implication. "*Her* Grizzled Baron" refers us back to the local suitors and suggests the irony that Emily Hardcastle may have preserved her high standards only for Death. "Stranger" is a quieter and less melodramatic reference to Death than "foreigner." "Gloomy halidom" is bookish; the less pretentious "castle in the gloom" preserves both the conceit of the suitor from 'away' and the forbidding mysteriousness of Emily's new condition. "Seal" brings in an association with the coffin and tomb. "Patter" is a fortunate suppression, for it invited an obvious pathos at the end and undermined the admirably controlled tone of the preceding stanzas.

"Armageddon," enlarged by a whole stanza in 1955, benefits from an increased clarity and precision. The confusion of the "patriarch" is more fully accounted for. Unable to distinguish between Christ and Antichrist, he delivers his complaint to the wrong one. This stanza of 1945,

> He sought the ear of Christ on these mad things,
> And in the white pavilion when he stood
> And saw them featured and dressed like twins at food,
> He poured in the wrong ear his misgivings,

is expanded in 1955 to

> He sought the ear of Christ on these strange things,
> But in the white pavilion when he stood,
> And saw them favored and dressed like twins at food,
> Profound and mad became his misgivings.

> The voices, and their burdens, he must hear,
> But equal between the pleasant Princes flew
> Theology, the arts, the old customs and the new;
> Hoarsely he ran and hissed in the wrong ear.

Now the confusion is more dramatic. "Hissed" is more strikingly consonant with the patriarch's bewildered state than "poured." However, not all of the changes are positive gains: "favored" seems no sharper than "featured"; and one whole line is wordy and pedantic—"Profound and mad became his misgivings."

Three words in "Winter Remembered" are changed in 1955. "Better to walk forth in the murderous air" becomes "Better to walk forth in the frozen air." "And where I went, the hugest winter blast..." becomes "And where I walked, the murderous winter blast...." "Frozen" is more definite and less shrill than "murderous," but the other changes are not meticulous improvements.

"Necrological" receives more attention in 1955. Three slight changes appear in the conclusion. The 1945 version:

> Then he sat upon a hill and hung his head,
> Riddling, riddling, and lost in a vast surmise,
> And so still that he likened himself unto those dead
> Whom the kites of Heaven solicited with sweet cries.

The 1955 version:

> Then he sat upon a hill and bowed his head
> As under a riddle, and in a deep surmise
> So still that he likened himself unto those dead
> Whom the kites of Heaven solicited with sweet cries.

The triteness of "hung his head" is eliminated, and the syntax is tightened. Like most of the changes for 1955, these are only modest improvements.

Some slight poems receive attention in 1955. "What Ducks Require" has three altered stanzas. In 1945 they read:

> This zone is temperate. The pond,
> Eye of a bleak Cyclops visage, catches
> Such glints of hyacinth and bland
> As bloom in aquarelles of ditches
> On a cold spring ground, and render
> A space supportable and a time tender.

The half-householders for estate
Beam their floor with ribs of grass,
Disdain your mortises and slate
And Lar who invalided lies,
Planting dangerous at the earth-heart
Where warm and cold precisely start.

Furled, then, the quadrate wing
From the lewd eye and fowler's gun
Till in that wet sequestering,
Webtoed, the progeny is done,
Cold-hatched, and from the blink of birth
Is native to the rhythmed earth.

This language is a curious mingling of precise, straightforward diction with labored, pedantic embellishment, like a stylized eighteenth-century treatment of nature from indoors, from inside a comfortable urban civilization. Revision does not diminish the anomaly of the academic treatment; the language is not better accommodated to the subject. But some slender improvements result. The first line here is made more logical: "The zone unready. But the pond...." Although the ducks do manage to nest and hatch their eggs in the temperate zone, the natural precariousness of it is enhanced by this change. The zone does not seem to be warm enough for them when they first arrive. "And render" is deleted and "a freak" substituted for it. Then the next line is changed to "A weathering chance even in the wrack." This provides an effective and highly relevant pun in "weathering"; and "freak" and "wrack" make a more interesting rhyme than "render" and "tender."

The last two lines of the next stanza become "The marsh quakes dangerous, the port/Where wet and dry precisely start." Again the rhyme is improved, and the strained diction of "earth-heart" is avoided. "Port" keeps alive the conceit of sailing that the poem begins with and that it will end with. The last two lines of the other stanza become "Cold-hatched the infant prodigy tries/To preen his feathers for the skies." They are still not outstanding lines. "Infant prodigy" is too obvious and too pedantic. But at least some eccentric phrasing—"blink of birth" and "the rhythmed earth"—has been suppressed.

One four-line passage in "Our Two Worthies" has had a mobile career. It was the third stanza when the poem first appeared in *Two Gentlemen in Bonds*. In 1945 it was placed just before the concluding stanza. Then in 1955 it was moved back to its original position. This work is so loosely constructed that it is hard to know where the passage works best.

"Of Margaret" has one altered stanza. The 1945 version:

> Soon must they all descend, there where they hung
> In gelid air, and the blind land be filled
> With dead, and a mere windiness unchild
> Her of the sons of all her mothering.

This whole poem is an exercise in preciosity, characterizing a woman who imagines her 'maternity' to consist of "all flowers and foliage." The major change is in the diction: pedantic and eccentric words—"descend," "gelid," "windiness"—are dropped. What most needed correcting is left untouched: the tautological line that follows "unchild," the most arresting word of this passage.

"Conrad in Twilight" has some unimportant changes. In the third stanza in 1945:

> Conrad's house has thick red walls
> And chips on Conrad's hearth are blazing,
> Slippers and pipe and tea are served,
> Butter and toast, Conrad, are pleasing!
> Still Conrad's back is not uncurved
> And here's an autumn on him, teasing.

Line two is changed to "The log on Conrad's hearth is blazing." Implausible direct address in line four is removed, but it is replaced by verbiage: "Butter and toast and tea are meant for pleasing." These changes are superficial, capricious, not positive improvements.

Two additions were made in 1955. "Vision by Sweetwater" and "Persistent Explorer" were resurrected from *Two Gentlemen in Bonds*. "Vision by Sweetwater" certainly deserves to be included in Ransom's *Selected Poems*; it is superior to several that he must have used to fill out the volume in 1945. The choice of "Persistent Explorer" is, however, more dubious. It reflects Ransom's persistent love of esthetic distance for its own sake, detachment when there is no strong emotion to be detached from. "Persistent Explorer" is a contrived parable of a modern dilemma: the desire for a supernatural sanction for existence but the incapacity to believe in one. An effigy of a character, the "explorer," debates with himself whether or not the sound of a waterfall conveys some sense of divinity. He tries to believe that there are supernatural overtones, but cannot. Still, he rejects the logical alternative of suicide and resolves to explore "another country." It is a frail poem, and the changes made in it for the 1955 edition are only minor adjustments of syntax.

Ransom's best poems are sterling products of a fidelity to emotional precision. Really excellent ones are few in number, and he had not overlooked any of these when he gathered his first *Selected Poems*. A fatal consequence of the interest that produced the best poems has been much unfruitful experimentation with detachment, poems that are stillborn because they have too little emotion or zest to be precise and decorous about. The most impressive fact about the revisions is that in 1945, and less spectacularly in 1955, Ransom not only reduced the sentimental phrasing and overstatement—obvious violations of his artistic code—but he was critical even of his peculiar kind of self-indulgence, his predilection for archaism and grandiloquence. In every version of *Selected Poems*, though, there have been whole representatives of a willingness to sacrifice power to esthetic distance, poems whose slightness is preordained by Ransom's attraction to motifs that have a built-in detachment: fanciful elaborations that lead to no illumination, no startling climax, no virtuosity of emotional control; strained little narratives that embody a transparent irony; thin caricatures. Guards against offensive emotionality are sometimes too patent and are themselves offensive.

Plausible characterization *can be* subordinated to an ironical idea, but "Miriam Tazewell" and "Of Margaret" do not redeem the experiment. Equally safe is the presentation of an undeveloped conflict, as "The Tall Girl" exemplifies. There is no tension created and no running of a course to a dramatic conclusion. "Man Without Sense of Direction" merely describes the frustrated condition of a man who is supposed to act like a lover but cannot. The poem is a cool report of the static conflict; it has no developing light, no accruing point. "Eclogue," a limp rehearsal of spiritual malaise and despair conducted by two stagy, stodgy people, is unrelieved by ingenuities of characterization, metaphor, irony, or language. Sheer whimsy—fancy made autonomous—is the source of many poems in *Chills and Fever* and *Two Gentlemen in Bonds,* and inevitably some of them have made their way into the *Selected Poems:* "Dog," "Her Eyes," "Survey of Literature," "Somewhere Is Such a Kingdom," and "Spiel of the Three Mountebanks."

III   *Resurrections and Altered Principles in 1963*

The *Selected Poems* of 1963 is larger than its predecessors because Ransom has been less selective than heretofore. He has plumped out his book by resurrecting more of his thin and tepid poems that are whimsical contrivances or that represent merely technical escapes from personal emotion. They are strange relics of a disinclination to reveal anything about the private self, a disinclination so formidable that it led him to invent fancifully, to construct vapid fictions that are literally detached from a strong emotional perception, the source and controlling motive of good poetry.

Revision of the perennials is less extensive and less dramatic even than in 1955. "Necrological" has one change: in the third stanza "The dead men" becomes "The dead." "Painted Head" has one change: in the fifth stanza "So that" becomes "Wherefore." The most significant change in "Old Mansion" is the utter deletion of the third stanza:

> Each time of seeing I absorbed some other feature
> Of a house whose annals in no wise could be brief
> Nor ignoble; for it expired as sweetly as Nature,
> With her tinge of oxidation on autumn leaf.

The fortunate loss of the awkward and pedantic first statement is counterbalanced by the regrettable loss of the second, one of the most memorable passages of the poem. Other revisions of "Old Mansion" are quite indifferent. In the fourth stanza "One need hardly imagine" becomes "One hardly imagines"; "Towers, white monoliths, or even ivied walls" becomes "Towers, arcades, or forbidding fortress walls"; "But sufficient state if its peacock *was* a pigeon" becomes "But sufficient state though its peacocks now were pigeons." In the seventh stanza, "Its exits and entrances" becomes "Its porches and bowers." In the eighth, "legend" becomes "wisdom." In the tenth, "wrapped" becomes "warped" (as in the original and the 1945 versions); "Who bids you" becomes "Who had bid me." In the twelfth, "foreign" becomes "dying."

What makes the 1963 edition so astonishing to old readers of Ransom is the *number* of whole poems that he adds: "Agitato ma non troppo," "First Travels of Max," "Prometheus in Straits," "In Process of a Noble Alliance," "Hilda," "Morning," "Old Man Pondered," "The Vanity of the Bright Young Men," "Master's in the Garden Again," and a radically modified version of "Prelude to an Evening" (an alternative to the standard version, which is still included). The first four had appeared in *Chills and Fever*, the next two in *Two Gentlemen in Bonds*.

We would not expect Ransom to have overlooked during all these years any poems equal to the superb quality of "Winter Remembered," "Blue Girls," "Bells for John Whiteside's Daughter," "Dead Boy," "Emily Hardcastle, Spinster," "Puncture," "The Equilibrists," "Antique Harvesters," "Judith of Bethulia," "Captain Carpenter," and "Prelude to an Evening." A new edition could be justified by less prodigious salvaging. But the revival of six mediocre poems from the early collections is an anomalous event in the career of a meticulous poet.

"Agitato ma non troppo" originally served as the dramatic introduction to *Chills and Fever*, and the whole poem was printed in italics. It was a terse, indirect announcement of an esthetic credo: this poet would no longer indulge in overstatement of emotion. Because it implies so boldly the radical change of method from that of the sentimental and shrill *Poems About God*, we can easily cooperate with the Ransom of 1924—suddenly finding a new direction—and we can be undisturbed by the slightness of a poem so well suited to the occasion. But, in the 1960's, its bareness is too apparent; the assertion of poetic principle is too dominant, too naïvely aggressive. A triumph over the abstraction would require more body, more richness, than Ransom supplies here; and the new revisions do not strengthen.

Contrivance on behalf of rhyme is the first ominous sign. After the bald assertion, "I have a grief," comes the strangely defensive line, "It was not stolen like a thief." Presumably, this line is a protest that the grief is authentic and private, that it is something felt, not something theatrically worked up. The formal, self-conscious denial creates an amusing irony; for, when the reader has finished the poem, he perceives that Ransom's treatment of grief is tame and bloodless, as academic as if it had been stolen. This line appeared in parentheses in the original version. Omission of the parentheses in the new version causes the reader logical trouble, for the next line, "Albeit I have no bittern by the lake," is syntactically related only to "I have a grief." Ransom's excluded bittern recalls the ravens and skylarks of some poets, the extravagant devices and portable props for creating atmosphere and telegraphing emotion to indolent readers.

Reference to Dante's authentic noble emotion is used to make Shelley's whimpering seem absurd and unmanly ("when the young heart was hit ... Shelley's reed sang tremolo"). Here is the purpose of the poem, to ridicule poetry based upon overt dejection and self-pity. Three trite distortions are presented as questions asked from an ironical perspective, by someone who expects from poetry the clichés of excessive pathos: how can a poem convey grief if the poet has not included an abandoned child or an old man frightened by his aging, or if the poet has not even dramatized himself as sleepless and anxious? The best is saved for last. "A leaf" shaken is a good figure for overt display of emotion, but it is unsatisfying as a climax to the poem. It is a verbal ending only, not a consummation of theme.

There is an incongruous mixing of stilted language ("Albeit," "brake," "None there has been," "assuredly") with natural, conversational language. Triteness mars each of the two new lines that are placed at the beginning of the poem in 1963, a regrettable lapse in a poem designed to ridicule standardized responses: "This is what the man said,/Insisting, standing on his head."

"Agitato ma non troppo" illustrates the self-defeating trait in Ransom's militant renunciation of directness. He calls attention to himself by the laborious ingenuity of method, by the haughty aloofness ("I will be brief"), and by the too-apparent determination to make a poem out of insubstantial materials. Toughness of detachment is so jealously guarded that no intensity grows. Our interest in this poem cannot exceed that of a literary historian, noting the counterdistortion in a rigid program of esthetic distance.

The method is a precarious one because the pursuit of subtlety requires self-imposed austerities that may either hopelessly impoverish a poem or call attention to a cold obsession with technique. A strange kind of Ransomian subtlety engenders the thin and vague portraiture to be found in "Hilda," "Morning," "Old Man Pondered," and "In Process of a Noble Alliance." Are these works not designed to avoid the grossness of illusion that makes a fictitious character stay in the reader's consciousness with some body, definiteness, and uniqueness? It must be that Ransom strives to create these anonymous people who can be so readily subordinated and assimilated to an idea; he deliberately produces insubstantial characters. The man and woman in "The Equilibrists" are like apparitions; the poem is saved because we are distracted from the thinness and vagueness of personality by a dazzling ingenuity of metaphor and attenuation of irony. In some poems, the successful distraction comes from an authentic gravity of language; but these four poems are not redeemed by any impressive compensating strengths.

"Hilda" and "In Process of a Noble Alliance" recall the admirable "Emily Hardcastle, Spinster." Ransom likes to make ironic drama out of a woman's choice between marriage and spinsterhood. In "Emily Hardcastle, Spinster"—a funeral ceremony presented under the metaphor of a marriage ceremony—the point is that Emily, having rejected the local suitors rather than compromise her standards, is now being wed to "the Grizzled Baron" and will be carried to his "castle in the gloom." "In Process of a Noble Alliance" reverses the terms of this motif: a marriage is described with the language and imagery appropriate to a funeral. This woman has been impelled to marry not by love but by hollow convention and thus she may be appropriately represented as 'dying.'

"Emily Hardcastle, Spinster" has a compressed richness. In four brief stanzas Ransom manages effective characterizations of both Emily and the narrator, who has admired her. A subtly attenuated irony justifies the bold metaphorical presentation: Emily may have preserved her extraordinary idealism only for Death. "In Process of a Noble Alliance," however, is unambitious; it is an abortive poem, with no course to run, no characterization, no climactic turn of irony, no development beyond the transparent idea that marriage without love constitutes death. Irony is presented heavily, banally; it is not allowed to overtake and surprise the reader. A too-obvious epithet, "queen of the House of No Love," signalizes abdication of the civilized poet's duty to please through powerful indirection. The ending is a pompous repetition of the idea made too apparent in the epithet: "A dirge then for her beauty, musicians!/ Not harping the springe that catches the dove." For a dove caught in the trap of worldliness, doomed to a cynical match, a dirge is more relevant than merry "harping," the music that accompanies a wedding.

"Hilda" has many symptoms of amateurism that encumber the delicate ambitiousness of purpose. Alliteration and rhyme seem not graceful and inevitable, but stolidly persisted in. The language suggests a resolution to embellish, perhaps a desire for elevation that has yielded only pomposity. Not very promising for the start is a laborious three-line circumlocution merely to announce that Hilda is about to be married:

> The dearest was the one to whom it fell
> To walk and wear her beauty as in a play
> To be enacted nobly on a great day;
> And stormily we approved the bosom-swell,
> And the tones tinkling. For her touch and smell
> I brought bright flowers, till garlanded she stood
> Scared with her splendor, as in the sight of God
> A pale girl curtsying with an asphodel.

This quotation is a compendium of vices incurred by Ransom's method. "Stormily" is bombastic; "tones tinkling," banal; "For her touch and smell," ludicrously precise. The only strong line, "Scared with her splendor, as in the sight of God," is diminished by the stylized, overembellished description that follows it.

Hilda is an Emily Hardcastle who, after succumbing temporarily and going as far as the altar, recovers her principles and refuses to take marriage vows. The narrator is Hilda's frustrated admirer, who wishes that she would look to him for comfort when she suddenly declines to go through with the ceremony:

> No, No, she answered in the extreme of fear,
> I cannot. On the dropping of those petals
> Rode the Estranger, scorning their sweet mettles,
> Blossoms and woman too; him she looked at,
> Not me the praiser; she was too honest for that,
> I was a clod mumbling, to catch her ear.

Strained and pompous expression continues: "in the extreme of fear," "scorning their sweet mettles." The use of "mettles" is a desperate concession to rhyme. Furthermore, it is a loose poetry that violates good sense by pointing out in this obvious way that the rejected bridegroom felt scorn for the flowers and the woman; we would hardly expect him to respond with joy and good will. "Estranger" is a ponderous archaism for "stranger," and its bookishness is not lessened by the inappropriate pun. If Hilda realized that she was dooming herself to spinsterhood by obeying this sudden impulse, she would naturally look after the outraged departing bridegroom; and, though the narrator would like to be acknowledged by her now, it seems farfetched to credit her with honesty. Ransom's indirect way shows her indifference toward the narrator, but the reader could assume that indifference since she had planned a marriage with another.

The next lines are the most vociferously 'poetic':

> The perished were the fairest. And now uprise
> Particular ghosts, who hollow and clamorous
> Come as blanched lepers crying, "Do not spurn us,"
> Ringing in my ears, wetting my eyes,
> Obsequious phantoms and disbodied sighs.
> Soon they are frightened and go fast; a smoke
> Which clung about my quincebushes, then broke,
> And while I look is smeared upon the skies.

Mutability is too obviously, too insistently, the emphasis here. The passage is marred by ineffective repetitions and by a belaboring of insubstantiality. Ransom tries to convey the dreamlike procession of dead people remembered, the mysterious recurring presence in the narrator's mind of people who have had claims upon his emotion. Aggressive rhetoric of insubstantiality —"blanched lepers," "Obsequious phantoms," "disbodied sighs" —does not provide an enriched sense of "Particular ghosts." In the middle of all this purple comes the jarringly flat statement, "Soon they are frightened and go fast."

This poem does not create the illusion that anybody lived through the experience described. Contrivance and heavy invention speak from each stanza. As preparation for the final stanza and the climactic attention to Hilda, the clamorous ghosts are described as "smoke" that "is smeared upon the skies." This obtrusive, imprecise image is supposed to convey the fading and blurring of all except Hilda. Nearly all of the last stanza is consistent with the obviousness and bloated rhetoric of the preceding ones:

> But Hilda! proudest, lingering last alone,
> Wreathing my roses with blue bitter dust,
> Think not I would reject you, for I must
> Weep for your nakedness and no retinue,
> And leap up as of old to follow you;
> But what I wear is flesh; it weighs like stone.

However, the concluding line tells what might have been made of this poem. This language is terse and unpretentious, yet carries subtle overtones. (It is the most brilliant revision in "Hilda" that Ransom made for the 1963 edition. The original ending offered no relief from the bombast: "But flesh hath monstrous gravity, as of stone.") The narrator realizes that, although Hilda lives in his memory more vividly than any other, he is aging and declining in his capacity to feel; and he is also experiencing the enormous difficulty of remaining loyal to a person who is not physically present. The new concluding line shows that a splendid idea for a poem has been sabotaged by wordiness and pomposity, by a language that *imposes* an esthetic distance and keeps the reader too completely detached from both Hilda and the narrator.

Ransom's gallery is composed mainly of timid characters, either paralyzed by an idealism that does not fit human existence or frightened by emotion. "Morning," carried over intact from the original, adds another thin and tepid portrait to the *Selected Poems*. Again a meager irony is stretched into the semblance of a poem. The mode of presentation is ingenuous; the narrative, too blunt. There is no fresh perspective, no compelling pretext for delivering the story. The destruction of suspense so early in the poem is ominous:

> Jane awoke Ralph so gently on one morning
> That first, before the true householder Learning
> Came back to tenant in the haunted head. . . .

This is a stolid preparation for Ralph's inability to live up to a lyric mood. Pedantic verbiage gives the sense of a lumbering narration: "true householder Learning" is not a deft conceit, any-way, but the echo of it in "to tenant" is sheer contrivance. The rest of this section has no memorable phrasing; the rhyme alone reminds us that this is a poem.

> He lay upon his back and let his stare
> Penetrate dazedly into the blue air
> That swam all round his bed,
> And in the blessed silence nothing was said.

Ransom usually avoids the earnest denotation of "Penetrate dazedly" and "blessed silence"; but he succumbs to it again with an adverb—"enchantedly"—in the following section, de-signed to present Ralph's lyric mood:

> Then his eyes travelled through the window
> And lit, enchantedly, on such a meadow
> Of wings and light and clover,
> He would propose to Jane then to go walking
> Through the green waves, and to be singing not talking;
> Such imps were pranking over
> Him helpless lying in bed beneath a cover.

Phrasing is not fresh enough to counteract the triteness of grass analogized to ocean waves, and the phrase "singing not talking" —more earnest directness—has little power to evoke a sense of Ralph's delightful temptation. An academic invention far away from feeling, the language lacks the bold, full commitment of romantic spontaneity. The nearest approach to it is the personifi-cation of the reckless impulses as pranking imps. (An excessively precise detail in the next line qualifies, however, even this abandon with a cautious decorum: "lying in bed beneath a cover.")

But no sooner does the poem rise to lyrical audacity than the heavy structural announcement is made: "Suddenly he remem-bered about himself,/His manliness returned entire to Ralph. . . ." The bluntness of this reversal recalls the heavy foreshadowing of "before the true householder Learning/Came back to tenant. . . ." Haste to conclude the poem seizes Ransom as he settles for the dull irony of "manliness" and illustrates it with the obvious com-parison of the self-conscious intellect to mechanics: "The dutiful mills of the brain/Began to whir with their smooth-grinding wheels...." Between this patch of mediocrity and the common-place ending appears the best line: "And the sly visitors wriggled off like eels..."; it is a good surrealistic rendering of the romantic impulses, though perhaps the contrast between organic claims and mechanical habituation is too overt, the juxtaposition of mills and eels too predictable. Nothing is left for the relentless conclusion to do but confirm the suspicion we receive from the second and third lines of the poem: "Morning" was not produced in a spirit of surprise and discovery, but was painstakingly worked out, made to accommodate a slender little idea: "He rose and was himself again./Simply another morning, and simply Jane."

"Old Man Pondered" is based upon a more compelling idea, and the design is toward a sharper climactic ending. The principal flaws are again clumsy narration and pompous language. An old man's singular and well-guarded demeanor is described, then accounted for by a speculation about his costly way of resisting despair: in his attempt to shut out from his consciousness the hate and scorn which he inspired in some people, he also had to exclude love. This analysis leads the observer to wonder about his own old age, specifically about what fate he is incurring by openly registering hate and transmitting love. It is an excellent conception.

However, the very title implies the starkness of this poem's construction. Ransom has the observer offer his help in interpreting, as he does in "Old Man Playing with Children," when, after the description of the old man playing games, comes the stodgy announcement, "But I will unriddle for you the thought of his mind." In "Old Man Pondered" the narrator first poses some questions:

> How are old spirits so dead? His eye seemed true
> As mine, he walked by it, it was as blue,
> How came it monstered in its fixed intent?

Then, just as flatly, he offers to interpret the psychology of the old man as reflected in his appearance: "But I will venture how." The speculation could have been launched into without this creaking narrative machinery. The language neither charms nor disarms. Trite and bookish by turns, it suggests a dogged effort to fabricate and worry the poem into a whole. Desperate academicism produces these phrases: "One who is fair and gentle," "and it was strange," "my most innocent," "monstered in its fixed intent," "Else those grim leers/Had won," "mild engine," "the lone sitter-in," "So hard consented," "a most immortal sorrow," "Thrice-pondered."

Metaphorical exhaustion sets in when a good figure, "many a bright-barbed hate," is echoed weakly by "a thousand spears." Clumsy syntax is the result of packing in words for the sake of rhyming efficiency: "The tenderest looks vainly upon him fell,/ Of dearest company." A simple meaning, "Burning to enter and destroy," is obfuscated by the insertion after "Burning" of "had smote against the optic gate."

This heavy and forbidding language insulates too well against any feeling. No intensity can accrue from rhetoric that is so artificial, that sounds so consistently like a parody of neo-Classical style. Ransom's formal language works best when he has committed his poem to a tone of gravity, as in "Antique Harvesters" and "Blue Girls." One of his recurrent strategies of subtle modernist technique, though, is to try to wrest an implausible advantage from the use of formal language, to exploit it in a whimsical, fanciful way as a guard against naïveté.

The title, "Prometheus in Straits," is meant to set the tone for a humorous, ironic poem by suggesting a Prometheus not in noble anguish but in a state of embarrassment. As the divine benefactor of mankind looks at the behavior of his protégés and at the civilization they have produced, he is forced to conclude that his faith in them was unwarranted, that he erred in befriending them. The weakness of this poem reflects Ransom's preoccupation with improbable indirection; it is the strategy that boomerangs the most often and the most noisily. Mannered pomposity of language is supposed to foster a subtle control, to differentiate the discourse from mere conversation and provide a kind of heightening and yet to induce an ironical effect by assimilating the pomposity to the subject and thus diverting it from the author himself. This technique is the fatal whimsicality that overwhelms so many of Ransom's poems, the misfired satirical impulse that produces doggerel.

What is selected to represent the cultural impoverishment is not very ingenious, and its presentation is not very clever. Between drinks men talk garrulously about politics, women "chatter/About old picture galleries and Westminster," and professors explicate so complicatedly that they lose the central meanings of books. Thus Prometheus concludes that where everybody is in competition to give learned explanation and expert opinion, no simple truths can flourish. The poem ends with his determination to build an altar to "the Unknown Man." This irony suggests that, as human beings have complacently allowed shallowness to prevail, they have left undiscovered and undeveloped some of their most valuable attributes, the ones that would have justified Prometheus' faith. Known Man is a failure, but Prometheus believes the shallowness was not inevitable.

Instead of the witty incisiveness called for by this fragile purpose, the language and elaborate feminine rhyme produce a heavy fancifulness that undermines any satiric potentiality. Overstatement and doggerel predominate, not subtle wit. The first stanza of the original version established the pattern for a wordy belaboring:

> Garrulous gentlemen on a veranda,
> Bibbers or non-bibbers of illicit potations,
> Rehearsing the acta and the agenda
> Of Republican or Democratic administrations,
> I am not committed to taking memoranda
> Culled from the lacunae of your cerebrations.

The poem was composed so exclusively of this fustian that the local revisions for 1963 do not make much difference, since they have to follow the commitment to pomposity:

> Windy gentlemen wreathing a long verandah,
> With tongues at the moments between illicit potations
> Assailing all the acta and/or agenda
> Of previous and/or present administrations:
> Observe me carefully jotting no memoranda
> Lest I seem to identify *your* wits with your nation's.

Some of the awkwardness and strain comes from the sheer choice of words; some, from eccentric syntax. "Wreathing" is so imprecise that the reader could not miss the rhetorical forcing. The cute moralistic phrase, "at the moments between illicit potations," is rudely wedged into place between what would be the natural syntax of "tongues" and "Assailing." When the reader arrives at the fifth line, he discovers that what he took to be description in the first four lines is a wordy, stilted direct address, a bombastic preparation for the pompous imperative, "Observe me." And the second stanza has more awkward syntax: "But now approaches a radiant band all spinster/Of spirits. ..." No more than the title is needed to identify the speaker of this poem, but a bald announcement appears in the fourth stanza, "Though I be Prometheus...." Quaint phrasing is resolutely continued: "my pious offices," "nullity is engendered," "my function concerns itself."

"First Travels of Max" reflects this strange willingness to sacrifice feeling and theme to tone. It is a curiously abortive poem, probably meant to be a dramatization of the evil that lies in wait for an innocent child. Reading it is a frustrating experience, though, because the meticulously prepared atmosphere has no significant action or illumination to justify it. Ransom is experimenting with a Gothic theme, but his fear of a naïve commitment to it impels him to undermine the horror with humor. A little boy ignores the prohibitions he has received against entering the forest and meets up with the Red Witch. The suggestion is that the encounter was inevitable, for she recognizes him and greets him familiarly, whereupon Max threatens to return when grown up and cut off her head. A humorous description of Max's bravado keeps the reader from too close an identification with him. Precise descriptions of the forest's interior have a made-up quality, a too-careful combination of horror and amusement. As in "Janet Waking," the humor imparts a condescension that forbids the reader to assume the child's perspective. The perspective of an adult is always present. So it is a tame Gothic performance.

The scrupulous guarding of tone effectually shuts out any feeling, if indeed Ransom began with a definite feeling. No culmination is reached. A brief stanza describes Max's fearful state as he returns home; then this longer stanza is the anticlimactic and muddling conclusion:

> Max is more firmly domiciliated.
> A great house is Van Vrooman, a green slope
> South to the sun do the great ones inhabit,
> And a few children play on the lawn with the nurse.

Max has returned to his play, and you may find him,
His famous curls unsmoothed, if you will call
Where the Van Vroomans live; the tribe Van Vrooman
Live there at least when any are at home.

Perhaps these lines are meant to suggest the complacent surface of existence that belies the boy's intuition of evil. Or do they imply a resiliency in Max that enables him to resume the peaceful life at home? They are a substitute for an ending, not a satisfying resolution of theme and tone. The materials of this poem might be suited to a ballad form like that of "Captain Carpenter" with its precise and concise language; but this sprawling and meandering form is wrong. Instead of building through a gradual accretion of relevant meaning, "First Travels of Max" moves diffusely, haphazardly; and it ends vaguely.

The poems added to the 1963 *Selected Poems* do nothing to enhance Ransom's reputation. There were already enough representatives of their kind in the 1945 and 1955 editions. Weak poems can only give more solidity to the eccentricities of the delicate poetics that Ransom persevered in earlier in this century.

In the preface to the new book Ransom says that he merely changed the title of "Tom, Tom, the Piper's Son," but the reworking is quite extensive. The greatly altered diction—mainly the removal of archaisms—and the persistent reliance upon denotative statement make "The Vanity of the Bright Young Men" a different poem on the same theme. The original Tom pushed a cart and sold wares, but the new version makes him bookish ("My familiars mostly are books"). Ransom may have tried to diminish the triteness in the idea of an economically deprived boy imagining he has received signs that he was a changeling.

The result is not a better poem, though, because the same implausible narrative device of talking trees is retained; it dooms the work to triviality. (Ransom is addicted to this bizarre overtness: he uses it in "Parting, Without a Sequel" and in "Vaunting Oak.") This new work is arresting not because it is a fresh improvement but because it signalizes a startling change of principle, a change that may be seen too in the most ambitious poems added to the 1963 edition, "Master's in the Garden Again" and the new version of "Prelude to an Evening." Directness—even overstatement—and flat assertion predominate. The reader's task of inferring is lightened; meaning is delivered explicitly; connections are made definite.

The first two stanzas of "Tom, Tom, the Piper's Son,"

> Grim in my little black coat as the sleazy beetle,
> And gone of hue,
> Lonely, a man reputed for softening little,
> Loving few—
>
> Mournfully going where men assemble, unfriended, pushing
> With laborious wares,
> And glaring with little grey eyes at whom I am brushing,
> Who would with theirs—

become in "The Vanity of the Bright Young Men"

> You think in my tight black coat I'm like a beetle.
> I never mind my looks,
> I'm removed, a boy reported not liking people,
> My familiars mostly are books.
>
> I go alone to assembly, but I'd go pushing
> Even to say my prayers,
> Glaring with cold grey eyes at whom I am brushing,
> Who would if they could with theirs.

In both versions the fictional perspective is implausible, but in the first one we sense an apparent effort to keep the expression from starkness. "Gone of hue" and "reputed for softening little" are not astonishingly rich phrases, but they do detain the reader longer than their successors. "I'd go pushing/Even to say my prayers" conveys an arrogance in the boy that undermines the Dickensian pathos of the old version. The push-cart implies inferior station and permits the reader to feel Tom's psychic isolation and his defensive, self-conscious independence.

Two stanzas of the 1955 version,

> Full of my thoughts as I trudge here and trundle yonder,
> Eyes on the ground
> Tricked by bird-flights or women to no wonder
> And no sound—
>
> Yet privy to great dreams, and secret in vainglory,
> And hot and proud,
> And poor and bewildered, and longing to hear my own story
> Rehearsed aloud—

are compressed into one:

> But afternoons I walk in the primal creation,
> In a spell, in a possible glory,
> Counting on Nature to give me an intimation
> Of my unlikely story.

Haste and expediency of narration are the motives behind these changes. Although the two stanzas have some directness, they nevertheless enlarge our sense of the boy's personality. The truncated one is not evocative; it is direct in a more obtrusive way than the first. It hints at a rigidity of structure. Walking "in the primal creation" and "Counting on Nature to give me an intimation" are very flat and hurried preparation for the description of the talking trees. Tom's *expecting* the trees to talk is an absurd refinement upon fancifulness.

The rigidity inevitably appears in the revision of the next stanza, from

> How I have passed, involved in these chances and choices,
> By certain trees
> Whose tiny attent auricles receive the true voices
> Of the wordless breeze—

to

> One time I went, by the luck of my chances and choices,
> Past certain Druid trees
> Whose leaves were ears and tongues translating the voices
> Hid in the muffling breeze.

"Druid trees" reflects the strained preconception, overstates the already offensive contrivance of the mystic communication. The eccentric phrase, "tiny attent auricles," is fortunately scuttled; but its replacement, "leaves were ears and tongues," has the kind of precision that creates preciosity.

Eccentric syntax and wordiness are kept in the next stanza. The old:

> And against me the council of spirits were not then darkened
> Who thereby house,
> As I set my boots to the path beneath them, and hearkened
> To the talking boughs—

and the new:

> Against me the counsels of spirits were not then darkened
> Though out of my vision or reach,
> As I set my boots to the path beneath and hearkened
> Unto phrases of English speech.

There is little to choose between these versions. The artificial syntax of the first line remains, and the strangely literal detail, "I set my boots to the path." The explicitness of "English speech" is amusing. Revisions for 1963 are mechanical; they do not have the charm and gracefulness that might have buoyed up this obdurate fancy. The lines have been tinkered with, worried over; but the meager little fiction of the proud, independent boy has not been transmuted into poetry.

The two major additions to the *Selected Poems* of 1963 are "Master's in the Garden Again" and the new, alternate version of "Prelude to an Evening." Both are recoilings from the unrelieved negativism of earlier poems. However, in the new ones Ransom incorporates the best lines of the old, and they solemnly, massively, remind the reader of the somber ends they formerly served and thus they make the new cheer seem like an inept application of cosmetic. Both poems are unconvincing; both are marred by an overt determination to ameliorate. There is something hollow and anticlimactic about the reclaimed Conrad's gesture of gaiety; and the curtailment of the splendid despair of the original "Prelude to an Evening" would be analogous to an attempt by Frost to diminish the horror of blankness in "Desert Places."

The final stanza of "Conrad in Twilight" is the only portion of the early poem in which the grim depletion of Conrad is skillfully implied. All the preceding lines sacrifice compassion to tone. The cool detachment and the mockery of an old man's infirmities are offensive. Ransom's coveted indirection is successful only in the precise description of the decline of the year, wherein the reader is impelled to feel Conrad's parallel decline as the consequence of a fierce mutability in the natural environment.

Most of this admirable stanza is imported into Section ii of the new poem; but, despite its unmistakable powerful implication, an overt explanation follows: "The show is of death. There is no defection." There is more of this underscoring, so uncharacteristic of Ransom's old principles. The cryptic statement of Conrad's, " 'The health of a garden is reason's burden,' " is made transparent when Ransom calls Conrad "the thinker." This humor is farcical, like that of the trite pun, "the fall of the year when it fell."

These are symptoms of the great difference in technique between this poem and "Conrad in Twilight." Ransom effects the metamorphosis with a stolid thematic purposefulness. The very beginning is as flatly unpoetic as a stage direction: "Evening comes early, and soon discovers/Exchange between these conjugate lovers." "Evening comes early" is a pedestrian way of starting a poem about aging, but "soon discovers/Exchange" suggests a hasty compromise with expression and narration. Then the anonymous people, effigies really, speak in a stilted way: " 'Conrad! dear man, surprise!' " and " 'Woman! intrusion!' " Stagy whimsicality holds the reader away, keeps him from any empathic involvement with the characters.

The only passage of genuine poetry is that borrowed from "Conrad in Twilight." I think Ransom's ambition is heroically to deny himself the advantages of moving characterization, lyrical language, startling metaphor—and to try to make meagerness yield him a low-toned and implausible esthetic victory. This poem resembles many of his early ones in the apparent effort to use whimsicality as a subtle technique. The usual result, however, is that the whimsicality keeps slipping into banality, as in this passage following the wife's practical suggestion that Conrad go into the house:

> "No," says the thinker. "Concede. I am here,
> Keeping guard of my garden and minding miasma.
> You're lonely, my loony? Your house is up there.
> Go and wait. If you won't, I'll go jump in the lake."

Each important stage of the narration is overstated, as though to prevent the reader from making a 'conventional' inference. Section iii begins with a flat explanation of Conrad's uncooperative behavior: "He will play out his mood before he takes food." Then follows an obvious linking of the decline of the foliage (leaves preciously described as "children") and the decline of Conrad:

By the bob of the Power the dark skies lower,
By the bite of Its frost the children were lost
Who hurt no one where they shone in the sun,
But the valiant heart knows a better part
Than to do with an "O did It lay them low,
But we're a poor sinner just going to dinner."

Ransom's objective is to convey a modest heroism in Conrad's refusal to give a stupefied assent to the naturalistic force that wears out everything, to assent by blandly accepting the ignoble consolation of an immediate dinner.

Conrad's gesture of defiance (against the "Power") is explicitly prepared for: "See the tell-tale art of the champion heart." The "art" consists of a frown, a rigidly set jaw, and a determination to be merry in the face of mutability even "if it damns him." This description is supposed to be comic hyperbole that will insulate against sentimentality and still let us see a courageous spirit. But the expression is not equal to the fragile design. Not comedy but nonsense results from this attempt at economy and rhyme, this personified set of a jaw: "The offense was raw, says the fix in the jaw."

Ransom tries to lessen the naïveté of Conrad's gesture by calling it a "pantomime blow." Eben Flood is convincing as a pathetic yet courageous victim of time. His effort to have a party, to be convivial in solitude, defines his sad plight but also reflects his splendid immunity from despair. Conrad's gesture of defiance and gaiety is unsupported by any convincing data. We can't get beyond the abstract reports of his mood and see or feel a human being. Doggerel can reinforce only the triviality of the poem's conception; it certainly cannot transmute it. Bareness of language, explicitness, and doggerel all undermine the lyric mood that is defiantly set against the natural force which wears out things and people.

In an explication accompanying the revised "Prelude to an Evening" Ransom gives his reason for reworking this poem. He had come to see it as too "vindictive," and he wished to "patch up the poem and save it; by saving the woman and the children from their distress; and of course by saving the villain too." This sounds ominous—a humanitarian concern for fictional characters. The admirable revisions of Ransom's earlier editions were governed by esthetic principles, not benignity. But this implausible motive asserts itself early in the new poem, with the second stanza, an entirely new one:

> You are my scholar. Then languish, expire
> With each day's terror and next week's doom
> Till we're twice espoused, in love and ruin,
> And grave but smiling though the heavens fall.

These lines are objectionable for two important reasons. As a matter of structure, they state the poem's theme too early and destroy suspensefulness. With this comforting explanation of the relationship between husband and wife, the powerful yet restrained horror of the original poem is suddenly canceled. And, most damaging of all, probably, considering Ransom's lifelong scrupulosity about tone, these lines have an easy didacticism: even though it may be true that people can manage their lives while refusing to deceive themselves about their intuitions of the quiet horror and terror in human existence, this passage softens the dread emotions, cheapens them. "Each day's terror and next week's doom" disposes of terrifying obsessions too blandly. "Smiling though the heavens fall" must be one of Ransom's most banal and sentimental phrases. The poem will not recover from this early, soothing injection of amiability.

The next seven stanzas of the original poem are retained, with some alterations of varying importance. An awkward participial phrase modifying "mind"—"Being as monsters in the dreams..." —gives way to the smoother construction, "Were monstrous only in the dreams...." An image for nightmarish fear, "the swarthy soldier," is softened and given an implication of monotony in "the same old soldier." This change is consistent with the idea that the woman's conscious psyche can quickly recover from the distortions of fearful dreams, but "swarthy" gave the image a greater energy and a melodramatic cast appropriate to nightmare.

Changes in two stanzas are distinct weakenings. The original speculation about how the wife's psychic state might parallel the narrator's, if "the night and day" of her mind were to be mixed, reads:

But now, by our perverse supposal,
There is a drift of fog on your mornings;
You in your peignoir, dainty at your orange-cup,
Feel poising round the sunny room

Invisible evil, deprived, and bold.
All day the clock will metronome
Your gallant fear; the needles clicking,
The heels detonating the stair's cavern.

The new version:

And now? To confirm our strange supposal,
Apparitions wait upon sunny mornings;
You in your peignoir commend the heaped oranges
Gold on the platter for cheeky children

But freeze at the turbulence under the floor
Where unclean spirits yawn and thrash;
The day-long clock will strike your fears;
The heels detonating the stair's cavern.

"Perverse" is better than "strange" to describe the man's effort
to project his obsession upon the wife. "There is a drift of fog
on your mornings" is a gentler and more mysterious mediation
between dream and consciousness. "Apparitions" says it too
bluntly, without connotation. The effects are subtler and richer
in the original stanzas: the paradox of behaving conventionally
while feeling the terrifying presences, the phantasmagoric heightening of trivial sounds. "Cheeky children," a lamentable pun,
works against the mood. "Where unclean spirits yawn and
thrash" is overstated, abstractly melodramatic. "Day-long clock"
is awkwardness posing as economy. The perfect word to suggest
persistent, obsessive awareness—"metronome"—freshly used as a
verb, is given up for the denotative word, "strike." "Deprived"
evil suggests a powerful reality that asserts itself after a long
period of more comfortable preoccupations; it has a much more
sinister implication than "the turbulence under the floor."

In the original version, innocuous household acts are made
precarious:

Freshening the water in the blue bowls
For the buckberries with not all your love,
You shall be listening for the low wind,
The warning sibilance of pines.

Ransom keeps this motif in 1963, but he revises for a more punctilious precision: "You listen for a low lost wind to awaken/ The warning sibilance of pines." The concluding stanza of the old poem is altered so that some of its best strokes are lost. These lines are the climactic extension of the wife's distraction:

> You like a waning moon, and I accusing
> Our too banded Eumenides,
> You shall make Noes but wanderingly,
> Smoothing the heads of the hungry children.

"Like a waning moon" is indistinct in meaning, but it probably suggests a sense of the gradual contraction and impoverishment of the sanguine hopes and comforts of a marriage in its early stages. This simile is good preparation for the "Eumenides," implacable cosmic forces that destroy the spirit and diminish hope. The last two lines swiftly capture the woman's vague, preoccupied behavior as a mother, going through the motions, disciplining the children absently, not concentrating upon them. The new version reads:

> Finally evening. Hear me denouncing
> Our equal and conniving Furies;
> You making Noes but they lack conviction;
> Smoothing the heads of the hungry children.

"Finally evening" is too much like a stage direction, and "Hear me denouncing" is stilted. The second line is a tame and wordy substitute for the splendid phrase memorable for both its sound and sense; "Our too banded Eumenides" suggests that they are too well organized and coordinated and too persistent. This strength of implication had to be diluted, certainly, to accommodate the four superadded stanzas:

> I would have us magnificent at my coming;
> Two souls tight-clasped; and a swamp of horrors.
> O you shall be handsome and brave at fearing.
> Now my step quickens; and meets a huge No!

> Whose No was it? like the hoarse policeman's,
> Clomping onstage in the Name of the Law.
> That was Me; forbidding tricks at homecoming;
> At the moment of coming to its white threshold.

I went to the nations of disorder
To be freed of the memory of good and evil;
There even your image was disfigured;
Then the boulevards rocked; they said, Go back.

I am here; and to balk my ruffian I bite
The tongue devising all that treason;
Then creep in my wounds to the sovereign flare
Of the room where you shine on the good children.

These lines constitute the "reversal" that Ransom speaks of in his explication of this poem. It is a mechanical one. Even with the new softenings and tamings the mood of evil is too titanic to be counteracted so handily. "A swamp of horrors" is rhetorical overstatement; it seems detached and contrived after the excellent data that quietly speak horror by showing the insidious penetration of evil to all the mundane household movements of the woman.

The reversal is effected by a very obtrusive narration, and a brilliant poem is emasculated by the expediency of good will. A verbal connection is made with the preceding stanza by the description of a "No" that does not "lack conviction." Then follows the artificial development by question and answer. Tightness and economy are abandoned in the sluggish effort to modify the strong negative mood, and the narration becomes blunt and mechanical:

Now my step quickens; and meets a huge No!

Whose No was it?

That was Me.

Capitalization of "Me" implies that the man's better self is judging the temptation to implicate the wife in the dreadful vision of evil. However, this vision suffers a strange diminution and discrediting with the use of the word "tricks"; this tone suits very poorly with the perverse projection. Furthermore, it makes the narrator seem like a paltry man, who must restrain himself from playing cruel little jokes on his wife. This rhetoric of diminishment occurs again with "I bite/The tongue devising all that treason." And probably the most regrettable undermining of the magnificent horror of this poem comes with the sentimental language of the very ending, in which the wife is said to "shine on the good children."

CHAPTER 7

Conclusion

AT A TIME when so much poetry is a revelation only of the author's exacerbated psyche we should appreciate the principled artistry of Ransom; he would not capitalize upon private agonies. If we first encountered Ransom in "Prelude to an Evening," we might suspect that his subject matter is some terrifying self-discovery of the kind Emily Dickinson often exploited. And who would ask for a greater degree of anonymity in execution? The poem is a dramatic realization, not a piece of raw confession. But it is Ransom's only successful venture into urgent introspection. Much of Robert Frost's poetry reflects a dramatic struggle between the romantic desire to stretch the boundaries of human life and a resolution to live wisely by not succumbing to illusion. These opposed interests give the poetry a tension; and, even through the most skillfully controlled presentation, the reader senses the poem's origin in strong personal feeling. Ransom is characteristically milder, more academic. Resignation comes easy to him. Then follow the intellectual pleasure of contemplating a little coolly what in human existence he has resigned himself to, and the esthetic pleasure of making an ingenious refinement upon detachment. Usually, whenever boldness appears, it is in technical execution—not in feeling and idea that involve personal risk, not in revelation of astonishing discoveries about the self.

If we confined our close inspection to the eleven best poems that Ransom has written, we might at first have the sense that variety paradoxically emerges from this self-imposed confinement within the techniques guaranteed to preserve anonymity. How different from one another appear "Dead Boy," "The Equilibrists," "Winter Remembered," "Antique Harvesters," "Captain Carpenter," "Judith of Bethulia," "Puncture," "Emily Hardcastle,

Spinster," "Blue Girls," "Prelude to an Evening," and "Bells for John Whiteside's Daughter." Yet, scrutinized closely, most of them reflect the dominance of theory and craft over the strong emotional perception that intrinsically defines a poet.

Experimentation did not carry Ransom beyond his preconceived dogmas. A meticulous reading of all the poems will diminish the sense of variety and will cause some disenchantment about Ransom's frequency of control over his favorite techniques. It will also lodge with the reader an annoying sense of Ransom's fussy eccentricities: his addiction to archaism and nostalgia, to innocuous drollery, to grandiloquence, to an anti-Victorian toughness, to flaccid irony. The persistence of these odd traits suggests that Ransom is usually in less danger of being carried away by emotion than by decorum. Many of his poems are so dominated by his severe practice of detachment that they seem like little exercises in different methods of subduing personal emotion. Frequently the people and the incidents that he invents are the terminus of his interest, not fictions subordinate to an illuminating perception or a powerful feeling. Symptoms of this autonomous fancifulness are the persistent repetitions of a remarkably few conflicts: desire for a passionate, committed life opposed by old age or emotional impotence; love versus honor; idealism versus disappointing realistic compromise or humiliating sense of limitation. Ransom's is largely a negative and timorous poetry, suffused with an uneasy feeling of mortality and emphasizing the great disparities between what people need emotionally and what they can have. The brave and reckless poems are exceptional, inharmonious with Ransom's standard production.

However, I think it does not work entirely to Ransom's disadvantage when we read all of his poems with care. Inevitably this scrutiny will reveal both the astonishing completeness of his esthetic purism and the incredible amount of strain and contrivance in much of his invention, but it will also create a new respect for his most successful poems. His greatest triumphs owe their permanent luster to the unlikely transcendence of his severe standards. He likes to work precariously, sparely; to forswear easy advantages; to steal a lyrical purpose from frozen parsnips; to disarm the reader by luring him into an outrageously comic story about a quixotic captain and then, with sureness and deftness, to leave him with a permanent vision of ambiguous human faith and folly; to enhance the pathos in the death of children by implausibly emphasizing their negative traits; to transfigure the erotic appeal of a beautiful woman by dramatizing the perverse political and military use that can be made of beauty.

As a critic, Ransom helped to define and establish rejuvenated Classical canons for poetry. As a poet, he worked scrupulously and originally within them. His best work is a brilliant consummation of the sophisticated esthetics that Poe struggled toward and that provincial America resists in all periods. The modern poetic sensibility must acquiesce in the prevailing milieu without surrendering devotion to the creative daemon. Cummings denounced the theory-heavy academy; and while Stevens, Frost, and Williams remained its friends, they kept their distance and haunted racier neighborhoods. Like many American poets in the nineteenth century and many more since World War II in the twentieth century, Ransom worked within its constrictions and suffered its tamenesses. His self-conscious reverence for principles of execution scholasticized his daemon.

Ransom is the most distinguished poet of his kind that America has produced. He is an academic poet, always seeking his most potent effect from the built-in paradox of his poetics: the intensification of feeling that comes from ascetic techniques. Academic or not, only a few poets of this century will add eleven works to the permanent tradition of English and American poetry.

Selected Bibliography

WORKS BY RANSOM

1. Books Written by John Crowe Ransom

Poems About God. New York: Henry Holt and Co., 1919.
Chills and Fever. New York: Alfred A. Knopf, 1924.
Grace After Meat. London: L. and V. Woolf, 1924.
Two Gentlemen in Bonds. New York: Alfred A. Knopf, 1927.
God Without Thunder. New York: Harcourt, Brace and Co., 1930.
The World's Body. New York: Charles Scribner's Sons, 1938.
The New Criticism. Norfolk, Conn.: New Directions, 1941.
Selected Poems. New York: Alfred A. Knopf, 1945.
Poems and Essays. New York: Vintage Books, 1955.
Selected Poems. New York: Alfred A. Knopf, 1963.

2. Books Edited by John Crowe Ransom

The Kenyon Critics. Cleveland: The World Publishing Co., 1951.
Selected Poems of Thomas Hardy. New York: The Macmillan Co., 1961.

For an exhaustive compilation of Ransom's essays up to 1948 see "John Crowe Ransom: A Checklist," by Robert Wooster Stallman in *Sewanee Review*, LVI (1948), 442–76.

Essays and Reviews by Ransom are listed in John M. Bradbury's *The Fugitives* (Chapel Hill, 1958).

STUDIES OF RANSOM'S POETRY

BEATTY, RICHMOND CROOM. "John Crowe Ransom as Poet," *Sewanee Review*, LII (1944), 344–66. In a rather wooden survey of Ransom's three early volumes Beatty indiscriminately mingles Ransom's excellent and mediocre poems, and ignores some of the best ones.

BRADBURY, JOHN M. "Ransom as Poet," *The Fugitives*. Chapel Hill: University of North Carolina Press, 1958. This chapter is too perfunctory a treatment of Ransom's poetry. Bradbury tries for a synoptic view of it without sufficient close scrutiny of particular poems. His analysis of technical effects is the most satisfactory feature. The use of "always," "all," "no," and "none" is distressing.

BROOKS, CLEANTH. "The Doric Delicacy," *Sewanee Review*, LVI (1948), 402–15. By a stolid determination to cooperate with whatever Ransom has written, Brooks converts weaknesses into strengths. He finds a parallelism between Ransom and Milton: both use Latinized diction and strive for esthetic distance. Possibly the impulse to eulogize Ransom keeps this critic from noticing the many poems in which a nonfunctional eccentricity of diction becomes an intrusive assertion of the private personality and is precisely what undermines Ransom's esthetic distance.

HOUGH, GRAHAM. "John Crowe Ransom: The Poet and the Critic," *Southern Review*, I (1965), 1–21. Hough undertakes an urbane and modest defense of the special kind of poetry Ransom writes, sympathizes with Ransom's persistence in his Southern heritage and his idiosyncratic and sophisticated transmutation of it into art. The generosity is too patent, however; for, when Hough tries to support his exaggerated claim for the importance of *Poems About God*, he fatuously compares "Dead Boy" and "Bells for John Whiteside's Daughter" with "Grace": "Yet these small, pathetic and understated deaths are the same Death as that of the hired man in 'Grace'. . . ."

JARRELL, RANDALL. "John Ransom's Poetry," *Sewanee Review*, LVI (1948), 378–90. This essay is too brief to fulfill its synoptic purpose, but it is a bold and sensitive 'appreciation' of Ransom's poetry. Jarrell largely redeems his strained effort at synthesis by sure, intuitive judgments about which are the best poems and by quick little descriptions of Ransom's elusive traits.

KOCH, VIVIENNE. "The Achievement of John Crowe Ransom," *Sewanee Review*, LVIII (1950), 227–61. Though too starkly organized, this essay registers important objections to Warren's unqualified assertions and arrives at defensible generalizations about Ransom's poetry through sensitive reading of some individual poems.

MATTHIESSEN, F. O. "Primarily Language," *Sewanee Review*, LVI (1948), 391–401. A defense of Ransom as a master of "good minor art" is weakened by indiscriminate praise for some of the slight poems. Matthiessen does not have Jarrell's unerring critical taste. However, he discusses well the versatile control that Ransom can exert through his special diction.

SCHWARTZ, DELMORE. "Instructed of Much Mortality," *Sewanee Review*, LIV (1946), 439–48. Schwartz points out a resemblance between Ransom and Stevens, and argues for an important difference. He cooperates with Warren's thesis, but with no reliance upon the glib concept "dissociation of sensibility." Sound generalizations are the essay's strength; the last part, an engagement of specific poems, is disappointing.

STEWART, JOHN L. "John Crowe Ransom's Poetry," *The Burden of Time*. Princeton: Princeton University Press, 1965. Stewart offers too little meticulous reading of Ransom's poems to support any judgments in this chapter. He has eccentric interpretations of "Necrological," "Spectral Lovers," and "Armageddon." The best discussion is of Ransom's limitations although, paradoxically, Stewart declares that Ransom has more than fifty excellent poems!

WARREN, ROBERT PENN. "John Crowe Ransom: A Study in Irony," *Virginia Quarterly Review*, XI (1935), 93–112. Facile and illusory comprehensiveness emerges from this effort to integrate the poetry of Ransom with his philosophical and critical views. The claims for irony are too rigid as Warren suggests that Ransom's particular kind of poetry is, like Eliot's, a private response to modern man's "dissociation of sensibility."

WASSERMAN, G. R. "The Irony of John Crowe Ransom," *University of Kansas City Review*, XXIII (1956), 151–60. This intelligent and incisive study of Ransom's irony might be juster if the thesis that "Ransom has a sympathy for his deluded characters" were not protected by excluding relevant poems from the discussion: "Miss Euphemia," "Here Lies a Lady," "Conrad in Twilight," "Parting at Dawn."

Index